HKS ARCHITECTURE

Published in Australia in 2010 by

The Images Publishing Group Pty Ltd

ABN 89 059 734 431

6 Bastow Place, Mulgrave, Victoria 3170, Australia

Tel: +61 3 9561 5544 Fax: +61 3 9561 4860

books@imagespublishing.com

www.imagespublishing.com

Copyright © The Images Publishing Group Pty Ltd 2010

The Images Publishing Group Reference Number: 828

National Library of Australia Cataloguing-in-Publication entry:

Title:	HKS architecture.
ISBN:	9781864703368 (hbk.)
Notes:	Includes index.
Subjects:	HKS Inc.
	Architecture—United States—History—20th century.
Dewey Number:	720.973

Editor/Director: Dan Noble

Creative Director: Shalmir Johnston

Art Direction and Graphic Design: James Frisbie

Editors: HKS Communications

Coordinating editor: Beth Browne

Production by The Graphic Image Studio Pty Ltd, Mulgrave, Australia

www.tgis.com.au

Pre-publishing services by Mission Productions Limited, Hong Kong

Printed on 150 gsm Quatro silk matt paper by Everbest printing Co LTD in Hong Kong, China

IMAGES has included on its website a page for special notices in relation to this and its other
publications. Please visit www.imagespublishing.com.

CONTENTS

Foreword		6
HKS Design Philosophy		8
Key Personnel		10
1	GREEN	15
2	HEAL	61
3	REST	139
4	PLAY	203
5	WORK	251
6	LEARN	279
7	LIVE	327
8	STUDY	341
9	APPENDIX	357

FOREWORD

Experts for change

HKS, then known as Harwood K. Smith, was first brought to my consciousness in 1979. The site was Austin, Texas, and the occasion was a Texas AIA Board of Directors retreat for strategic planning. I had just turned 30.

The reason I recall it so vividly still today is that at the time I was struck by the sensation that this was a meeting of dramatic opposites. I was visiting from Minnesota, thrilled to escape the sub-zero weather, and Texas was wonderfully warm by comparison. This was but the first contrast I experienced.

The meeting was populated with architects who seemed very confident and determined about making bold changes as well as those who were uncertain that change was needed at all. Some were from big firms, some from small. Some were quiet in the midst of the boisterous majority. There were serious people ("Our licensing laws are threatened like never before!") and playful people (who could spin yarns akin to those of Garrison Keillor on *A Prairie Home Companion*).

This was the exhilarating atmosphere in which I recognized the watchful expectation for a Dallas firm that insiders referred to as HKS.

In 1981, I was appointed to the national AIA Board of Directors. Fortune was on my side, as the tool used to assign seating for meetings of the far-too-large board of directors was the alphabet. This is how I came to be seated next to Texas director William Caudill at our first Washington meeting. Caudill was a founder of the Houston firm CRS.

Ideas on architecture

HKS was emerging as one of the bellwether firms Caudill talked about. It is quite possible even that he foresaw its evolution, which – a decade later – would lead it to become a nationally significant firm. As for me, I came to understand HKS and appreciate it better as history unfolded in the coming two decades.

Moving forward into the early 1980s, I recall HKS leaders Joe Buskuhl and Ron Skaggs, who had a vision of growth and emergent world-class strength

for the firm. Buskuhl was one of the leaders of the AIA Large Firm Round-table, and Skaggs would soon become AIA president. Buskuhl led a watershed meeting of the roundtable to formulate its voice in the larger national organization. Skaggs presided over the AIA during a trying period, and his leadership was often tested. It was during this time that AIA addressed many of its organizational issues.

Simultaneously, HKS was blossoming as a firm and a brand, taking a position as a national and international role model and earning the respect of architecture and construction professionals alike. The firm was much talked about by client groups, including the American Chamber of Commerce and the Business Roundtable. As I reflect on that period, I see that clients discovered the greatness of HKS before many in the profession did.

The rise of HKS continued throughout the 1990s and into the 2000s. Under the current guidance of the leadership team of Chairman and CEO Ralph Hawkins and Executive Vice Presidents Nunzio DeSantis, Craig Beale and Dan Noble, the firm has reached an elite status. Each is quick to recognize that the firm's international success is due to the collaboration between all members of the firm, including principals, vice presidents, associates and Forum employees.

Hawkins began serving as president in 2002. His leadership and vision have allowed the firm to continue to expand in an international economy while maintaining its best-place-to-work practices. Under his direction, HKS has successfully expanded its services into new markets and locations. The firm's presence spans the globe with 24 offices worldwide.

More than 15 years ago, DeSantis formed the firm's hospitality practice with the goal of creating memorable, one-of-a-kind hospitality experiences. Most recently, he led the efforts to grow a high-impact hospitality design firm along with John Hill and Bob Glazier. This merger has allowed HKS to rank as a worldwide leader in hospitality design.

As director of HKS Healthcare, Beale has furthered the practice's overall organization, mission and focus including introducing the Clinical Solutions & Research and the Medical Equipment Planning and Technology groups. He has been instrumental in the development and expansion of the firm's overall design services across the United States, Europe, the Middle East and Latin America.

Noble's efforts as design director have helped to create a framework that promotes design excellence for the entire firm. His role as executive vice president allows him to continue these efforts in an amplified leadership role.

None of these professionals would have referred to it in that way perhaps, but the firm that Harwood K. Smith had guided to local levels had reached the national and international strata. HKS has become a firm recognized for quality service, delivery and design excellence. Awards and media attention are common. The architecture profession also recognized HKS as a best practice firm.

The future is innovation

HKS stands firmly on a platform of strength as envisioned by leaders of the last decade of the 20th century and the first decade of the 21st century – if not by Harwood K. Smith himself. Moreover, we see depth of services tuned to the challenges of our time: master planning, programming, project management, structural engineering, interior design and other services offered worldwide along with architecture. And with this expansion and success come even higher expectations.

In 2008, I had the opportunity to facilitate a strategic planning session of the firm's 120-plus partners and principals. This impressive assemblage demonstrated energy, enthusiasm and vision. Not only were fresh ideas shared, but big advances were made improving the fundamentals – the quarterbacking, blocking and tackling of design excellence. HKS is further developing its global practice and with multiple value drivers, some new, some legacy. It is a brand of relevance, of distinctiveness and a firm often referred to as having an extraordinary business sense. HKS is leading in building information modeling, integrated project delivery and sustainable design. When the firm's leaders discuss the challenges of today and of the future, they take the opportunities brought about by change and insert them into a metaphorical zipper of professional practice. They are adaptive to change and they stick with innovation. The consistent strength of their performance surprises and puzzles their skeptics.

Embracing opposites

Seventeenth-century philosopher Blaise Pascal wrote, "A man does not show his greatness by being at one extremity, but rather by touching both at once." As you read this book and look at the pictures, you will see that HKS is not at one extreme or another. It is not avant garde. Nor is it traditional. HKS presents a mix of design, service and project delivery strength in multi-dimensional ways. And it has become a respected form-giving firm, too. When I asked HKS employees and clients about the most-admired buildings of the firm, they pointed to dozens of architectural works. Clients have noted that the firm is possessed with strong talent that can and often does lead to innovative facilities and strong solutions.

You will further discover in this book that there are many buildings of distinction in the HKS portfolio. Sometimes this shows immediately on the skin (Fidelity Investments in Westlake, Texas); other times it is in the unseen sustainable principles that break old paradigms of energy use metrics (Letterman Digital Arts Center in San Francisco). The firm stays current; its buildings are intentionally innovative.

And, this is a resilient firm. Operating through three economic recessions, HKS has emerged from each one a stronger organization. This is true in the minute details of professional skills, in energetic leadership, in operational attitudes of service and in taking the responsibility to show us a way out of the one-sided extremism that has limited much of the architecture of our time.

Finally, HKS has demonstrated that great work can happen in large firms. It has shown us an architecture that works along with occasional miracles. Just think about its hospitals and the lives that are saved there (George Washington University Hospital), the learning at schools that give rise to future generations of wisdom (Texas A&M Hagler Center) and the sublime facilities it has created that have enhanced the human condition and will most certainly continue to do so as this century unfolds. The true hour of its work is yet to come.

James P. Cramer, Hon AIA, Hon IIDA, CAE
Chairman, The Greenway Group; Founding Editor, DesignIntelligence; President, Design Futures Council; and Former Chief Executive, American Institute of Architects

HKS DESIGN PHILOSOPHY

At HKS we Listen, Innovate and Deliver.

This is not simply an empty tagline but a description of an integrated, collaborative design process. We begin every project free of any preconceived notion of the final design outcome. We have the means to help our clients understand the key issues behind multiple potential solutions and provide them with the tools needed to determine value for themselves.

Listen – Successful design begins with an open relationship and dialogue between the client and design team. We have to be active, engaged listeners to fully understand our clients' goals and help discover potential solutions. Our design solutions are not mandated by a prescriptive idea of style, but thoughtfully built to fit the individual needs and goals of each client as we help guide the team along a trajectory of mutual discovery.

Innovate – Research and investigation are the lifeblood of innovation. Our sustainability and R&D groups constantly revitalize the firm with fresh ideas and new approaches to design elements and methods of construction. We work with our professional consultants on all of our projects to leverage progressive thought and develop innovative solutions. This rigorous analysis and research, coupled with an emotional connection to our work, allow us to deliver fully developed concepts that evoke a sense of place and improve people's connection to our buildings and each other.

Deliver – Delivery is critical to the overall success of a project and one of our notable strengths. At its most basic premise, project delivery is about communication. We work around the world and manage projects on some of the most complex designs imaginable. Through this varied and substantial experience we have developed protocols that allow our designs to mature while coordination between team members is realized.

To do this effectively, all members of the team must understand the design concept and work to support its intentions.

Process

Develop a concept – We define a concept as a thought, inspiration or intended experience that can provide guidance and give aesthetic direction for all design disciplines throughout the entire design process.

Cohesive design begins with a clear intention. We need to understand the key issues you are trying to address and what kind of response you are intending to evoke from those who interact with the facility. We believe a rational exploration into a facility's needs and a wholly developed concept embraced by all team members will result in buildings that exude a sense of harmony and enjoy an organic relationship with the site. Done correctly, this process encourages a balance between the poetic and the pragmatic that allows our work to be both passionate and grounded.

Design workshops – By organizing design workshops with the entire team at the beginning of the process, we are able to define the key issues and set in motion an agreed upon direction by the entire team – including the client. This direction can always shift and respond to evolving concepts, but the "big idea" remains as the overarching design organizational tool. As the design discovery process unfolds, periodic design reviews keep the project on track and communicate to the team continual refinements in the direction of the solution while preserving the quality of the initial concept. These reviews encourage cross-fertilization between market sectors and enable firm-wide consistency of design quality.

Studio organization – Our teams are organized into studios of 15–25 people led by design principals and designers with proven experience who are responsible for the project from initial conception through the construction phase. This affords our projects the attention of a boutique firm with the resources of one of the largest firms in the world. Artificial boundaries are not superimposed on studio members – anyone can generate a great idea. In fact, the collaboration between interns and principals on equal footing is encouraged, creating a dynamic, energized environment where thoughts build upon each other and become greater than the sum of the parts. This level playing field allows us to develop ideas from a fully-leveraged talent pool, encouraging a collaborative spirit within the entire firm while benefitting each individual project.

Collaboration – We believe that the most successful, full-bodied design solutions arise from a collaborative design process that begins with a holistic approach to problem seeking. Before we can solve a problem, we have to identify the core essence of what we are trying to solve. Problem seeking and solving is a dialogue of discovery through respectful interaction with the industry's most inventive multi-disciplined minds. We are considered thought leaders in many building sectors and can "dig deep" to understand our clients' business in a disciplined, focused fashion extending these lessons learned into our other sectors. This cross-pollination of ideas leverages our collective knowledge and allows us to become a valuable asset to our clients. We understand our clients' business needs and interpret these needs into a design response that establishes the building as an ally to the business at hand.

Stewardship

Sustainability – Thoughtful design begins with good stewardship of the environment. Our integrated design process encourages exploration of sustainable design concepts from the beginning of every project, with all design team members actively engaged in a mutually understood design direction. We believe this is the most effective path to successful sustainable design. Our in-house sustainability group is dedicated to providing environmental and sustainable leadership for each of our projects.

Civic responsibility – We are obligated as neighbors in our communities to contribute in a positive fashion to the built environment and understand our buildings' position within the greater context. We recognize a building's impact on its immediate surroundings and the environment as a whole, and we continually work to be responsible stewards of our neighborhoods and our planet.

Social responsibility – Good design can improve the human condition. Whether our solutions help decrease medical errors in a hospital by creating a more healing supportive environment, or show an understanding of how people move through enormous crowds at sporting events, or craft a soothing sense of place and respite for vacationers, the environments we shape have a direct effect on the people who interact with them. The skillful execution of a deliberate and thoughtful design will contribute to a building's success and create timeless design solutions born of a sense of place that enrich the lives of people who interact with them.

Executive Committee

Chairman and CEO

Ralph Hawkins, FAIA, FACHA, LEED AP [1]

Executive Vice President

Nunzio DeSantis, FAIA, LEED AP [2]

Executive Vice President

Craig Beale, FAIA, FACHA, FACHE, FAAHC, LEED AP [3]

Executive Vice President

Dan Noble, FAIA, FACHA, LEED AP [4]

Management Council of Principals

Noel Barrick, AIA [5]

Bobby Booth, AIA [6]

Ron Gover, AIA, ACHA, LEED AP [7]

Billy Hinton, AIA, LEED AP [8]

Dan Jeakins, AIA, LEED AP [9]

Chuck Means, AIA, ACHA [10]

Fred Roberts, AIA [11]

Jeffrey Stouffer, AIA [12]

Bryan Trubey, AIA [13]

Principals

Eddie Abeyta, AIA, LEED AP

Tom Amis, AIA, LEED AP

Danny Babin, AIA, LEED AP

Joe Buskuhl, FAIA

Davis Chauviere, AIA, LEED AP

Kosal Chittoor, AIA, LEED AP *

Matt Clear, AIA, LEED AP

Doug Compton, AIA, LEED AP

Melanie Cornell

Jess Corrigan, AIA

Ron Dennis, FAIA, FACHA

Bob Farrow, AIA, FHFI, LEED AP

Francis Gallagher, RIBA †

Robert Glazier, AIA

Francisco Gonzalez, AIA

Todd Gritch, FAIA, FACHA, CBO, LEED AP

Roy Gunsolus, AIA, LEED AP

Ernie Hanchey, AIA

Tom Harvey, FAIA, MPH, FACHA, LEED AP

John Hesseler, AIA, LEED AP

John Hill, AIA, LEED AP

Kerry Hogue, AIA, LEED AP

1
2
3
4

5
6
7
8
9
10
11
12
13

* HKS India Design Consulting Pvt. Ltd.   † HKS Architects Limited   ‡ HKS Arquitectos S. de R. L. de C. V.

Tom Holt, AIA

John Hutchings, AIA, LEED AP

Paul Hyett, PPRIBA, Hon. DArt, Hon. FAIA†

Steve Jacobson, AIA, LEED AP

Jeff Jensen, AIA

Richard Johnston, AIA, LEED AP

Mark Jones, AIA

Kirk Krueger, AIA, CCCA

Rick Lee, AIA, LEED AP

Bob Martineck, AIA, LEED AP

Owen McCrory, AIA, LEED AP

Mike Menefee, AIA, LEED AP

Norman Morgan, AIA

Alan Palmer, RIBA†

David Prusha, AIA

Ricardo Rondon, RA‡

Nick Shapland†

Ron Skaggs, FAIA, FACHA, FHFI, LEED AP

Joe Sprague, FAIA, FACHA, FHFI

Mo Stein, FAIA, FACHA

Craig Stockwell, AIA

Kirk Teske, AIA, LEED AP

Jeff Vandersall, AIA, LEED AP

Craig Williams, AIA, ESQ.

Mark Williams, AIA, LEED AP

Senior Vice Presidents

Doug Atmore, AIA, LEED AP

Kevin Bailey, AIA, LEED AP

Johnny Baize, AIA, CCCA, LEED AP

Gary Baker, AIA

Carl Beers, AIA

Betsy Berg, ACHE, MSHA

John Bienko, AIA

Bob Billingsley, AIA, LEED AP

Tom Briggs, AIA

Marc Budaus, AIA, ACHA, LEED AP

Rex Carpenter, AIA, LEED AP

Lorenzo Castillo, AIA

Glenn Clarke, IIDA

Bob Cline, AIA

Byron Donelson, AIA

Brendan Dunnigan, AIA, LEED AP

Brian Eason, AIA, LEED AP

Frank Effland, AIA

Eduardo Egea, AIA, CAAPPR

Jeanne Erickson, AIA, LEED AP

Jerry Fawcett, AIA

Leslie Hanson, AIA

Don Harrier, AIA, CDS, LEED AP

Jeff Haven, AIA, LEED AP

Jeff Hill, AIA, LEED AP

Cliff Horsak, AIA

Dennis Hughes, AIA, CCCA

Mark Hults, AIA, LEED AP

Teresa Hurd, AIA, LEED AP

Dan Jansen, AIA, LEED AP

Bruce Johnson, AIA, LEED AP

Larry Johnson, PE, LEED AP

Linda Keenan, AIA

Michael Kim, AIA, LEED AP

Shannon Kraus, AIA, ACHA, LEED AP

Joe Laakman, AIA

Jeff LaRue, AIA

Angela Lee, AIA, LEED AP

Larry LeMaster, CPA

Anita Linney-Isaacson, AIA, LEED AP

Michele MacCracken, AIA, LEED AP

Trish Martineck

Maria Martinico, CID, IIDA, LEED AP

Peter Mason, AIA, LEED AP

Brian McFarlane, AIA

David Meyer, RID

Rodney Morrissey, AIA

Michael Nicolaus, AIA, LEED AP

Bob Piatek, AIA, LEED AP

Craig Rader, AIA, LEED AP

Evelyn Reyers, AIA, LEED AP

Robert Robbins, AIA, LEED AP

Brad Schrader, AIA, LEED AP

Steve Shearer

Ray Smith, AIA, CCCA, LEED AP

Tim Solohubow, AIA

Brent Sparks, AIA, LEED AP

Brian Sullivan, AIA, LEED AP

Kevin Taylor, AIA, LEED AP

Steve Terrill, AIA

Larry Tuccio, AIA, LEED AP

Mark Vander Voort, AIA, LEED AP

Mike Vela, AIA, CDT, LEED AP

Dave Vincent, AIA, ACHA, LEED AP

Neal Vincent, AIA

Jay Waters, AIA, LEED AP

John Wix, AIA

Penny Wright, AIA, LEED AP

Frank Yin, PE

Luis Zapiain

Andy Zekany, PE, SECB

Vice Presidents

Lorrie Adair, AIA, LEED AP

Dennis Agren, AIA, CCS, LEED AP

Neil Alcorn, AIA, MBA

Jim Alotto, AIA

Eric Antalek, AIA

Kenneth Apel, AIA

Dan Arrowood, AIA

Marcia Ascanio, AIA, LEED AP

John Avdoulos, AIA

Tony Bartho, FAPM, CPM, RIBA, LEED AP

Bernita Beikmann, AIA

David Beller, AIA, LEED AP

Gary Blazzard, AIA, LEED AP

Kathleen Bolton, AIA

Michel Borg, AIA, LEED AP

Jonathan Borrell, AIA

Trip Boswell

Peter Braun

Ron Briggs, RA, CSI, LEED AP

John Brooks, AIA

Jeff Brown, AIA, CCCA

Frances Bruns, IIDA

Steve Buell, AIA, CDT, LEED AP

Jeffrey Bush, AIA, LEED AP

Virgil Campaneria, AIA

Brian Cargill, AIA

Camilo Carrillo, AIA, LEED AP

Percy Chang

Sze Chong, AIA, LEED AP

Irene Clark, AIA, ACHA, LEED AP

Owen Coffee, AIA

Brad Collard, AIA, LEED AP

Dan Considine, CCCA

Gary Cox, RA

Jeff Cox, AIA, CSI, LEED AP

Bill Craig, AIA, LEED AP

Jason Crist, AIA, LEED AP

Sean D'Artra, AIA, LEED AP

Iris Dates, IIDA, LEED AP

Greg Davenport, PE, LEED AP

Julie Del Angel, CID, LEED AP

Brenda Devling

Mark Donahue, AIA, LEED AP

John Dreiling, AIA, CSI, CCS

Chet Emmett, PE

Jennie Evans, RN, LEED AP

Ralph Evans, FAIA

Steven Evans, AIA, CSI, LEED AP

Bill Filip, AIA

Charlie Ford, AIA

Jack Ford, AIA, IDSA

Rick Franz, AIA, ACHA

Loretta Fulvio, CID, IIDA

Debra Garner, RN

David Goodenow, AIA, CDT, LEED AP

Chris Grasby, RIBA, FRSA†

Enrique Greenwell, Intl. Assoc. AIA, LEED AP

Terry Hajduk

Jason Hale, AIA, LEED AP

Tom Harry, AIA, LEED AP

Kyley Harvey, AIA

Andy Henning, AIA, LEED AP

Shae Hensley, AIA, LEED AP

Ricardo Heria, PE, LEED AP‡

Jane Ho, RIBA†

David Holland, AIA, LEED AP

Joe Don Holley, AIA, LEED AP

Richard Horrow

Michael Hurd, AIA

Gary Inglis, RIBA, ARIAS

Zach Jekot, AIA, LEED AP

Vinson Johnson, AIA

Shalmir Johnston

Christopher Jones, AIA

Carol Kartje, AIA, IIDA, LEED AP

Jonathan Kelley, AIA, LEED AP

David Kellogg, MBA

Mark Kiszonak

Frank Kittredge, Jr.

Derek Knowles, AIA

Greg LaGrega, AIA, LEED AP

Jesses Laird, AIA, LEED AP

Rod Lanham, AIA

Keith Lashley, AIA

Khoi Le, LEED AP

Paul Liptak, AIA, LEED AP

Steve Lopez, AIA, LEED AP

Dan Luhrs, AIA

Johnny Luttrull, CCCA

Jack Madsen, AIA, CDT

Mike Mamer, AIA, LEED AP

Carlos Marcet, AIA, ACHA, LEED AP

David Marshallsay, RIBA†

Bryan McMath, AIA, LEED AP

Charles McNeel, AIA, LEED AP

Seth Meltzer, AIA

Ron Meyer, AIA

Emanuel Mikho, PhD

Dan Miles, AIA, CDT, LEED AP

Michael Miller, AIA

Scott Miller, AIA, FACHA

Brad Mitchell, AIA, CDT, LEED AP

Jim Montemayor, AIA, LEED AP

Erik Moorhead, PE, LEED AP

Andrew Morgenthal, AIA, CDT, LEED AP

Bryan Mounger, AIA, LEED AP

Raymond Neal, AIA, LEED AP

Brian Nelson, AIA

Mark Nine, AIA, LEED AP

John Niziolek, AIA, LEED AP

Michael Novendstern, AIA

Fred Ortiz, AIA

Chris Osborn, AIA

Mark Overton

George Pappas, AIA

Debajyoti Pati, PhD, FIIA, LEED AP

Gordon Peck, AIA

Claudia Peres

Mike Rich, AIA, LEED AP

Jeff Richardson, RA, LEED AP

Terry Ritchey, RN, BSN, MBA

Michael Rogers, AIA

Sergio Saenz, ARQ, Intl. AIA

Robert Sampson, AIA, ACHA, LEED AP

Paul Sawyers†

Chad Scheckel, AIA

Todd Scherle, AIA, CCCA, LEED AP

Jason Schroer, AIA, LEED AP

Jerry Sherman, AIA

Mark Simpson†

David Skaggs, AIA, LEED AP

Bill Smith, AIA, LEED AP

Sid Smith, AIA

Cliff Snyder, AIA, EDAC

Karl Sonnier, AIA, MBA

Bill Stimson, AIA

Kathy Stuhler

Tom Stuhler, AIA, LEED AP

Jay Suever, AIA, LEED AP

Roger Sutherland, CPA

David Thomas, AIA

Eric Thomas, AIA, LEED AP

Mark Timm, RID, IIDA

Patrick Treadway, AIA, LEED AP

Tina Triche, AIA

John Tumino, AIA

Michael Ufer, AIA, LEED AP

Ede Vessey, PE, SE

Julie Volosin, IIDA, LEED AP

Lamont Wade, AIA, CDT

Dennis Walo, AIA

Laura Walters, CCCA

Alex Wang, AIA, LEED AP

Michael Wells, AIA, LEED AP

Michael Wensowitch, AIA

James Whitt, PE

Marsha Whitt

Greg Whittemore, AIA, LEED AP

Walt Wilson, AIA, CDT, CSI

Jeffrey Woosley, AIA, CSI, LEED AP

Lisa Yan, AIA, LEED AP

Karen Yeoman, CCCA

Associates

Olga Acosta, RID

Laura Aguilar, AIA, CCCA

Bill Alexander, AIA

Robin Allen, RN

Julianne Amacker, CDT

Cindy Andrews, PHR

Jennifer Andrews, AIA, LEED AP

Daron Andrus

Keny Anglim, LEED AP

Michael Ayer, AIA

Bradley Barnhart, AIA, LEED AP

Jonathan Barrick, AIA, LEED AP

Kathryn Barry, AIA, LEED AP

Glenn Barton

Jesse Beard

Teresa Beers, LEED AP

Kerry Bennett, AIA, LEED AP

Preston Bennett, AIA, LEED AP

Jonathan Bethune, AIA

Ryan Blaylock

Shea Bond, AIA, LEED AP

Anne Boudreau

Cindy Boyer

Patrick Brady, AIA

Meredith Brelo

Rupert Brown, AIA

Robert Bruder, AIA, LEED AP

Kim Bruffy, CID

Bruce Burnett, LEED AP†

Mark Buskuhl

Jay Caddell, AIA, LEED AP

Denise Calehuff, IIDA, LEED AP

Stevan Caronia, AIA, LEED AP

David Carpenter, AIA, CDT, LEED AP

Byron Chambers, LEED AP

Sergio Chavez

Aaron Chayovan, LEED AP

Laurence Chiang, AIA, LEED AP

Gaurav Chopra, Assoc AIA, IIA, LEED AP*

Thomas Chuparkoff, AIA, LEED AP

Jack Clark

Steven Cloutier, CCCA

John Coles

Elizabeth Conway, LEED AP

Darren Copeland, AIA

Shelley Corson

Tim Cotter

Travis Cowie, AIA, LEED AP

Heather Crosswhite, AIA, CDT, LEED AP

John Curtis, AIA, CDT, LEED AP

Vincent Czarnowski, AIA

Alejandro Danel, RA, LEED AP‡

James DeLavan

Beckie Dennis, AIA, LEED AP

Jamie Dorsey, CID

Steve Doyel

Mike Drye, AIA

Robert Du

Tina Duncan, AIA

Beau Eaton

John Elledge, AIA, LEED AP

Michael Estes, AIA, LEED AP

Lance Evans

Gina Ferrer

Stacie Flowers

Bradley Foster, AIA, LEED AP

Steve Fotiu, Assoc. AIA

Matt Franklin, CDT

Karen Funke, CPSM

Tracy Gay

Daniel Getz, PE

Martha Gibson

Melinda Goodroe, AIA, LEED AP

Emily Gossett, RID, IIDA, LEED AP

Tatiana Guimaraes, Assoc. AIA, CREA

Rebecca Haas, IIDA, LEED AP

Jason Haigler, AIA, LEED AP

Becca Hall

Kara Hanson, LEED AP

Chris Hardwick, AIA

Scott Haugh, AIA

Jason Henson, AIA, LEED AP

James Herckt, AIA, LEED AP

Michael Hessert, AIA

Laura Hild, AAHID, CID, IIDA, LEED AP

Henry Hill

Dave Hoadley, CDT

Lori Holtkamp, CID, IIDA

Tim Hopkins

Beckie Howell†

Lawrence Hughey, AIA, CCS, LEED AP

James Hutchinson, BMET

Alan Jackson

Andrew Jaeger

Scott Jarrette, CCCA

Chris Jenkins, AIA, LEED AP

Lisa Jones, CID

Brian Junge, AIA

David Kozack

Gordon Kwong, LEED AP

Kathy Kyle

Sunitha Lakshman

Nancy Lang

Mary Gaye Lewis

Alexander Ling, AIA

Rich Love, SPHR, CCP, CBP

Jamie Luce, MCP

Mike Mabry, AIA, LEED AP

Ray Mabry, AIA, LEED AP

Christian MacCarroll, LEED AP

Michael Malone, AIA, LEED AP

Jason Maloney, AIA, LEED AP

David Mangum, AIA

Ryan Martin, Assoc. AIA

Blake Marvin

Heath May

Luciano Mazza†

Clare McGirr, ACA†

Jennifer McKeel, AIA, LEED AP

Channing McLeod, AIA, LEED AP

Todd Medd, AIA

Kara Melton, PHR

Eric Messing, AIA

Aimee Middleton, AIA

Kalinka Mikel, RA, LEED AP‡

Robert Miller, AIA, LEED AP

Sandra Miller, IIDA, LEED AP

Jennifer Moen, AIA, LEED AP

Shane Mommers

Sylvia Morehart

Dana Muller, AIA, LEED AP

Chris Mundell, AIA, CSI, CDT, LEED AP

Robert Napper

Eric Nelson, CCCA

Shawn Newman, AIA, LEED AP

Todd Nicholson, PE

Stamati Nicolakis, AIA, LEED AP

Kevin Nikiel, AIA

Ann Noble

Peter Oliver

Martin Ortega, AIA, LEED AP

Shirley Overlay, CCCA

Alfonso Padro, ARB, RIBA†

Michael Penrose†

Dan Phillips

Roger Phillips, AIA, CDT, LEED AP

Clint Pickett

Juan Pineda, RA, LEED AP‡

Diane Pittman, AIA, CCS, CCCA, LEED AP

Brian Polinsky, AIA, LEED AP

Heather Potter

Brian Pounds, AIA, LEED AP

Nick Price, AIA, LEED AP

John Pypa, AIA

Kidd Quick, AIA, LEED AP

Ben Rees, RIBA†

Scott Revier

Daryl Robinson, RA, CSI, CCS

Augusto Rodelo MacGregor

Alfredo Rodriguez

Kenneth Roman

Richard Rucksdashel

Sheila Ruder, AIA, EDAC, LEED AP

Barbara Ruppel, AIA

Jess Sargent, CID, IIDA, LEED AP

Rachel Saucier, AIA, LEED AP

Karla Seelandt, AIA, LEED AP

Travis Sheets, CID

Daryl Shields

Michael Shihadeh-Shald, AIA

Lance Smith, AIA

Patrick Smith

Steven Smith, AIA

Thomas Smith

Hazel Springer

Connie Stanton, CIW

Anice Stephens

Walter Stephens

Christina Straughan

Michael Strohmer, AIA

Steven Stroman, LEED AP

Paul Strudwick, RIBA†

Laura Thielen, R.Ph., IIDA, LEED AP

Michael Thompson, AIA

Dulce Torres-Fuentevilla, RA, Intl. Assoc. AIA, LEED AP

Norio Tsuchiya, AIA, LEED AP

Erik Tuomy, CDT, LEED AP

Emir Tursic, AIA

David Urling, CID

Steve Valenta

Gregorio Vasquez

Jennifer Wagner, CID

Melissa Wallis

Greg Walston

Joan Warrick

Janine Watson

Jennifer Widmer, AIA

Sharisse Williams, AIA, LEED AP

Timothy Winger, AIA, LEED AP

Onney Wongmelert, AIA, LEED AP

Kelly Wood

Chenyue Yuan, AIA, LEED AP

1 | GREEN

Vision Dallas	16
W Hollywood Hotel & Residences	22
Milwaukee Palomar	26
Capital Health System Mercer Hospital	30
Woodruff Health Sciences Center	34
Hall Financial Office Tower	38
RadioShack Riverfront Campus	42
The Palazzo Resort Hotel Casino	48
Sabre Holdings Headquarters	50
St. Mary's/Duluth Clinic	56

VISION DALLAS

Design/Completion: 2009
Location: Dallas, Texas
Client: Dallas Central CDC
Size: 1 million square feet

This new inner-city community is founded on sustainable living and regenerative design solutions. To maximize open space, living units are concentrated into two residential towers. The form and orientation of the towers optimize daylighting and prevailing summer breezes. At the base of the towers, an inclined park provides space for food production, habitat and a gravity-operated water-scrubbing system that uses native flora for water purification.

Enhanced geothermal energy exceeds the energy demand, and additional power is harvested via an extensive photovoltaic array on the south façade of the north tower. The resulting concept harnesses the power of the natural and sustainable systems, resulting in a net power provider of carbon-free energy.

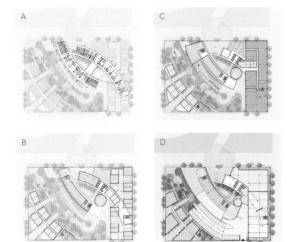

A. typical lower level
B. park live level
C. park work level
D. ground level

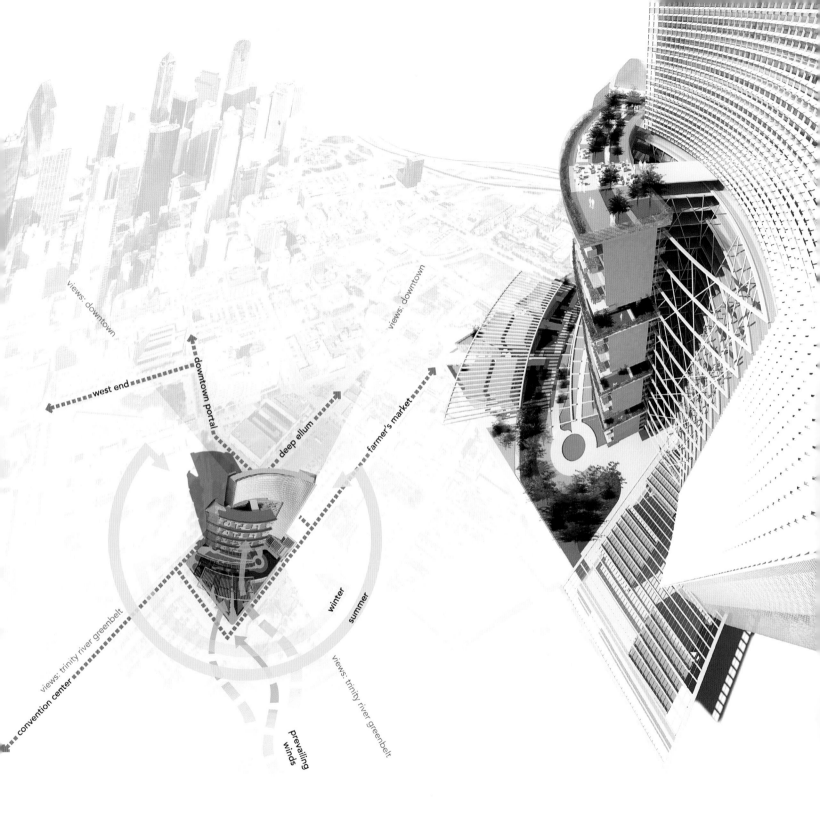

views: downtown

west end

downtown portal

deep ellum

views: downtown

farmer's market

convention center

views: trinity river greenbelt

winter

summer

views: trinity river greenbelt

prevailing winds

W HOLLYWOOD HOTEL & RESIDENCES

Design/Completion: 2009
Location: Hollywood, California
Client: Gatehouse Capital, HEI, Metropolitan Transit Authority
Size: 1.1 million square feet

The W Hollywood Hotel & Residences is designed to revitalize and contribute to the transformation of the historic Hollywood Boulevard through bold architectural expression and a memorable guest experience.

Seeking LEED certification, the project – located in a high-density, mixed-use urban environment – contains 300 luxury hotel rooms and 145 condominium residences with private, rooftop dwellings that provide an urban oasis for guests and residents. Specialty features include private film junket suites, upscale retail, fine dining, a boutique spa and a sky lounge.

The W partakes in the Hollywood Boulevard experience through the welcoming extension of the lobby's red carpet to the Walk of Fame, dynamic façades clad with super graphics and the building's signature element – the iconic, floating sky bar. The W is sited to complement the cityscape and provide easy access to the MTA transit plaza. The sense of scale, patterns and rhythms of the nearby buildings – including the Taft Building and the Pantages Theatre – are respectful and complemented with a modern expression.

An icon of modern living, style and sophistication, the hotel will serve as a gateway to the Hollywood Historic District. The elements of the movie industry that have so powerfully left a mark on the identity of the Hollywood community, and Western society as a whole, will be unmistakably represented in the architecture of the new luxury, mixed-use development.

MILWAUKEE PALOMAR

Design/Completion: 2008

Location: Milwaukee, Wisconsin

Client: Gatehouse Capital

Size: 750,000 square feet

The Milwaukee Palomar Hotel and Residences captures the spirit of Milwaukee's sense of place through a vertical mixed-use experience. The project showcases the city's character, strength and progressiveness through a bold expression of form, material and composition.

The tower, comprising a 185-room hotel and 76 upscale condominiums, is positioned at the site's primary intersection. The urban edge of the city is reinforced as the tower rises boldly above a two-story podium of metal and glass.

The hotel, located in the lower section of the tower, is clad with a unified monolithic stone-like expression executed in architectural precast. A public park is an integral design element at the foundation of the tower, while retail spaces line the base of the entire city block, synergizing the streetscape with public function.

As a climatic response to the city's harsh winters, the tower is clad with a metal shield-like skin that wraps the upper portion of the north, south and west façades. The tower takes advantage of its Lake Michigan views with a large curtainwall façade expressing maximum visibility for the residences. A distinctive feature is the sky bar/lounge, which is a floating observatory overlooking the park below and the city skyline beyond.

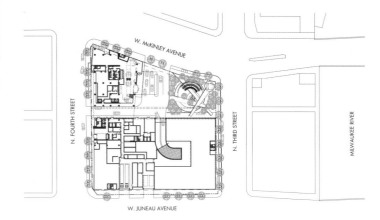

CAPITAL HEALTH SYSTEM MERCER HOSPITAL

Design/Completion:	2011
Location:	Hopewell Township, New Jersey
Client:	Capital Health System
Size:	925,000 square feet
Association:	ARRAY Healthcare Facilities Solutions

Capital Health System Mercer Hospital at Hopewell Township combines the comforts of the hospitality trend in healthcare with the technological demands of modern medical care, the latest in patient and staff safety and a commitment to sustainability.

Located on 165 acres of rolling farmland, the acute care hospital is strategically situated to take advantage of the natural terrain, views and wetland areas on the site. Its modern forms, grounded within a solid framework of materials drawn from regional traditions, create a rich and inviting facility that nurtures the emotional and spiritual wellbeing of patients, visitors and staff.

Elements of the architecture complement the pastoral character of the site, echoing the soft lines and relaxed informality of nature as seen in the broad curves and irregular rhythms of glass that punctuate the building façades. Gardens surrounding the facility merge with the landscape, anchoring the building in the natural environment and providing places of respite. Rooftop gardens create additional retreats for patients and staff.

Many of the project's sustainable features strive to preserve the integrity of the natural landscape by exceeding open space requirements, conserving water by using captured rainwater for irrigation, protecting the site's natural water flows and restoring native plants.

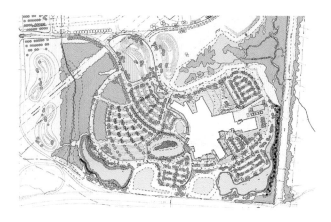

WOODRUFF HEALTH SCIENCES CENTER

Design/Completion: 2007
Location: Atlanta, Georgia
Client: Emory University
Size: 480,000 square feet
Association: Ayers Saint Gross

The Woodruff Health Sciences Center will provide a single location to access world-renowned expertise in a variety of disciplines. Designed for LEED-Silver certification, sustainable aspects include green vegetation walls on two sides of the 730-car parking deck and extensive use of natural light.

The building is composed of four clinic pavilions, a corner office pavilion and an internal pedestrian galleria. This flexible module includes repetitive structural bays as well as horizontal and vertical circulation for patients and staff. Sensitive to the bustle of Clifton Road, a public garden separates the building while reinforcing Emory's commitment to a pleasant, pedestrian-friendly, walkable campus.

At the main entrance, a glass canopy, paving patterns and landscaping lead guests to the main fountain, which anchors the galleria at the south. Landscape elements and glazed walls create a seamless transition between healing spaces and the exterior.

Natural light permeates throughout the entire clinic. Large areas of glazing provide panoramic views of the gardens and campus. Light also pours into the galleria and the parking structure lobbies, guiding visitors from the moment they arrive.

Exterior proportions and rhythm relate to the historic original campus architecture. The new clinic incorporates materials historically expressed throughout the campus. Additionally, the selection of contemporary building technology – such as double-glazed curtain walls and perforated sun screens – ensure the clinic operates in a sustainable manner.

horizontal rhythm vertical rhythm

HALL FINANCIAL OFFICE TOWER

Design/Completion: 2007

Location: Frisco, Texas

Client: Hall Financial Group

Size: 397,500 square feet

The Hall Financial Office Tower expresses a modern sense of identity and visual distinction for an office user seeking uniqueness and corporate sophistication. Located in a park-like setting, the tower is targeted to receive LEED-Silver certification.

Building users connect with nature through a modern composition of landscape elements enhanced with modern art. The lobby, a double-volume transparent space, connects with the park as the outdoors visually becomes part of the lobby experience. An over-scale sculpture, which reaches 150 feet into the sky, is a focal point from the lobby to the landscape beyond.

The office tower, which fronts a high-speed interstate, evokes a strong sense of visual identity through a tapering penthouse roof. The penthouse provides executive office tenants a signature interior design expression with a large triangular volume of space and distinct structural framing piercing the interior void. A 6,500-square-foot roof terrace offers seating areas surrounded by landscaped gardens, sculptural artwork and views overlooking the rolling cityscape – allowing opportunities to host unique corporate events and gatherings. Events can also be held outside on the main level due to the building's lush and eco-friendly landscape defined with outdoor patios, unique water elements and artistic sculpture gardens.

RADIOSHACK RIVERFRONT CAMPUS

Design/Completion:	2005
Location:	Fort Worth, Texas
Client:	RadioShack
Size:	900,000 square feet

RadioShack Riverfront Campus accommodates approximately 2,400 employees and features 600,000 square feet of state-of-the-art office space and 300,000 square feet of support and employee amenity space. Aggressive incorporation of sustainable and environmentally responsible design strategies earned the campus the distinction of the largest project in Texas to qualify for LEED-Silver certification when occupied.

Responding to its urban site and suburban character, the headquarters incorporates two different public faces. The urban side reflects the Fort Worth central business district with liberal use of red brick, Texas limestone and a fountain running the length of a plaza for all citizens to enjoy. The suburban side faces the Trinity River with walls of low-E glass, walk-out balconies and a wide greenbelt featuring native grasses and plants that extend to the river's edge.

RadioShack identified process refinement and productivity improvement as significant goals. Recognizing that the workplace can have a significant influence on these goals, HKS focused on an open-plan solution with collaborative teaming and commons areas, along with wireless computer network connections that enhanced interaction among teams supporting creative, customer-centric business solutions. With underfloor air distribution, each of the campus' 30,000-square-foot office floors incorporates collaborative, open work settings including those for the most senior officers.

THE PALAZZO RESORT HOTEL CASINO

Design/Completion:	2008
Location:	Las Vegas, Nevada
Client:	The Palazzo
Size:	7.4 million square feet
Association:	James R. Rimelspach, Architect, LTD. and Wilson & Associates

The Palazzo Resort Hotel Casino, located on the Las Vegas Strip, is certified by the U.S. Green Building Council as the largest green building in the world.

More than 40 percent of the Palazzo's footprint is open to the outdoors with extensive pools, a fountain, terrace and planted areas to enjoy. Artificial turf, drip irrigation and moisture sensors are located in planted areas, resulting in a 75-plus percent reduction in irrigation needs and swimming pools are warmed with solar pool heating systems.

However, some of the biggest environmental innovations at The Palazzo are inside each of the resort's 3,000-plus guest suites. Air conditioning controls in suites automatically set back by several degrees when guests are not present and reset to the desired temperature upon return. Also, a master light switch is located next to each door, allowing guests to turn off all of the suite lights in just one movement. In addition, interior plumbing fixtures use 37 percent less water than conventional buildings.

Today, the facility saves 10.1 million kilowatt hours of energy, 41 million gallons of water and 19,000 therms of gas annually. In its first year of operation, more than 16.4 million pounds of CO_2 were prevented from entering the atmosphere.

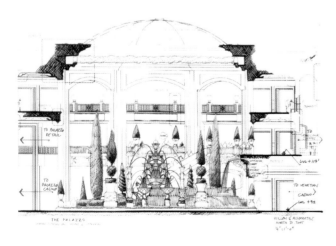

SABRE HOLDINGS HEADQUARTERS

Design/Completion:	2001
Location:	Southlake, Texas
Client:	Sabre Holdings, Inc.
Size:	475,000 square feet

Sabre wanted to create an economical, sustainable headquarters for its 1,700 high-tech employees. The resulting two-building complex situated on a heavily wooded site was one of the first and largest projects in the United States to receive LEED-Silver certification. The two facilities are part of a master planned 157-acre, 2-million-square-foot, 10-building campus.

This project is a benchmark in the Dallas area for energy efficiency, water conservation and indoor environmental quality. Its environmentally conscious exterior skin includes native Texas stone, aluminum, low-E glass and precast concrete. A water retention pond provides site irrigation.

The pedestrian-friendly campus encourages employees to access buildings via landscaped walkways. The public areas and amenity spaces of the contemporary headquarters are planned along a "main street" spine that links the two buildings.

The main lobby is a light-filled, high-tech space with a 28-foot-high ceiling adorned with a glass and metal grand stair, a floating curved ceiling plane, Venetian plaster wall finishes and polished concrete floors. The open ceilings expose the building's operational components, creating an energetic, collegial work environment appealing to the young workforce.

Employees have a wide array of meal choices available in the servery along with walking trails and a fitness center on the site.

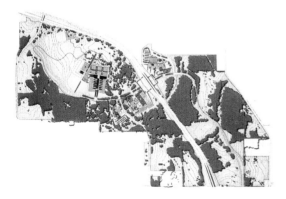

ST. MARY'S/DULUTH CLINIC

Design/Completion: 2006
Location: Duluth, Minnesota
Client: St. Mary's/Duluth Clinic Health System
Size: 245,000 square feet

The Duluth Clinic First Street Building promotes a healthy environment for patients, staff and the community by following sustainable design principles and by using its natural setting to create a relaxed, calm environment.

The client's enlightened approach to the design process acknowledged that buildings fundamentally impact the health of their occupants and the environment at large. The building is one of the first LEED-Gold certified healthcare facilities in the United States. The project incorporates sustainable design strategies that reduce energy and water use, reduce environmental toxins, reduce and recycle wastes, improve indoor air quality and support the healing process.

The outpatient services addition to a downtown medical center houses a comprehensive cancer center, a digestive health center, a diagnostic imaging center and laboratory, as well as pediatric, internal medicine and OB/GYN clinics.

Located on a redeveloped urban brownfield on a south-facing hillside overlooking Lake Superior, the building's organization gives patients access to daylight and panoramic views of the lake to put them at ease through a connection to the natural surroundings. An interior palette of blues, greens and grays, accented with wood finishes, contributes to a relaxed atmosphere by reflecting the soft hues of the surrounding northern Minnesota forests and lakeshore.

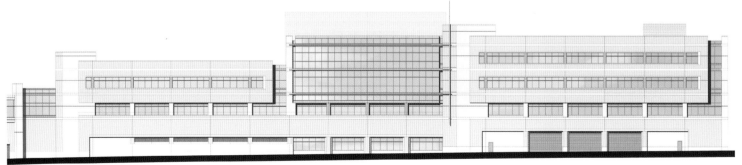

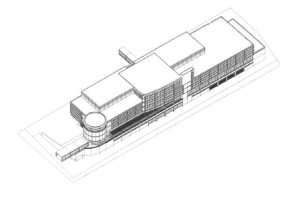

2 | HEAL

Nelson Mandela Children's Hospital   62

National Taiwan University Cancer Center   64

Bassett Army Community Hospital   66

University Hospitals Ahuja Medical Center   70

Karbala Teaching Hospital   76

Federal University of Health Sciences   80

Danat Al Emarat Woman's and Children's Hospital   84

American British Cowdray Cancer Center   88

Enze Medical Center   94

Abbott Northwestern Heart Hospital   100

Christus Muguerza Tuxtla Hospital   104

Al Qudra Healthcare Medical Campus   106

Royal Children's Hospital   110

Salem Hospital Regional Health Services   114

Lynn Cancer Institute – Harvey & Phyllis Sandler Pavilion   120

Phoenix Children's Hospital   124

King Hussein Cancer Center   128

Dubai Cancer Center   132

Northern Batch Hope Hospital   134

NELSON MANDELA CHILDREN'S HOSPITAL

Design/Completion:	2009
Location:	Johannesburg, South Africa
Client:	Nelson Mandela Children's Fund
Size:	322,000 square feet

The design for the new Nelson Mandela Children's Hospital (NMCH) celebrates a welcoming, park-like setting while creating opportunities for the community's public engagement with the hospital. The 322,000-square-foot facility is organized around a "Main Street" spine that runs east to west, connecting the patient bed building and the diagnostic and treatment areas of the hospital. Bordering a large lawn, this main thoroughfare also serves as a gathering space for many seasonal community celebrations. Animals can be brought in from the local zoo, as appropriate, to exterior viewing areas for the young patients. Special areas are provided for community garden clubs to contribute flowers and herb gardens, and museums are offered exhibit space along "Main Street" for the entertainment and education of patients.

The soft forms of the patient wings not only provide a welcoming image but maximize views to the outdoors and natural breezes. The bed buildings are raised above grade to create shaded and protected outdoor areas for children's playing and dining. A 200-bed hospital with the capacity to increase to 300 beds, the NMCH also provides an 80-unit building to accommodate the patients' parents. In addition, by taking advantage of the site's contours, public parking for 600 cars is covered by a landscaped park at street level.

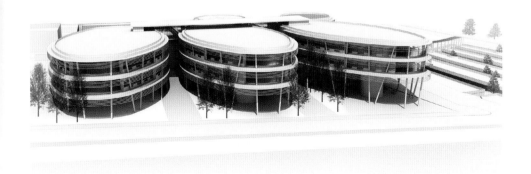

NATIONAL TAIWAN UNIVERSITY CANCER CENTER

Design/Completion: 2014

Location: Taipei, Taiwan

Client: National Taiwan University

Size: 426,500 square feet

The mission of this comprehensive, state-of-the-art cancer center is to become the number one cancer hospital in Asia, serving the entire Pan-Chinese community fighting cancer through HEARTS – Hope, Education, Affection, Research, Technology and Services.

The Chinese Yuen, a circular shape that symbolizes wholeness, perfection and harmony between people and Mother Nature, was used to define key elements and zones of care. It also allowed the symbol of the circle to be both literal and expressed throughout the design. The entire concept is built around unity.

Simple yet elegant, the design unifies and creates an integrated environment that delivers the best in healthcare. The Yuen itself is manifested as a "Light of Hope" circular atrium – used to inspire as it brings natural light into imaging and treatment areas that are often overlooked. This atrium is the anchor point for the three-story medical mall that serves as a physical and symbolic organizing element, as it separates the inpatient tower from the ambulatory and research spaces.

The naturally sunlit mall and open atrium space provide comfortable seating and positive distractions for patients and families. Most ambulatory services are located along this mall, such as chemotherapy and specialty cancer clinics. The treatment spaces and clinic waiting areas open into landscaped healing gardens incorporated into the site environment.

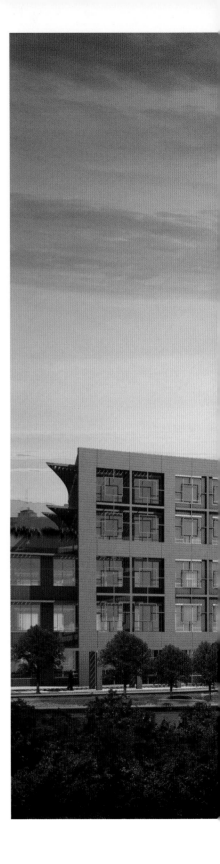

BASSETT ARMY COMMUNITY HOSPITAL

Design/Completion: 2006
Location: Fort Wainwright, Alaska
Client: U.S. Army Corps of Engineers, Alaska District
Size: 260,000 square feet
Association: Wingler Sharp Architects & Planners, Inc.

The Bassett Army Community Hospital replaces a 300-bed facility that was originally built in 1951, serving United States troops from all over the world. The facility is organized into three distinct pieces including the green, crescent and anchor wings.

The green is a representation of the village green and serves as a meeting space and path that connects the destination within the facility. The green is the central focal point of the building and a mediator between the two wings. The crescent wing houses inpatient facilities clinics, while the anchor wing houses building support and additional clinics.

Inside the facility, colored lighting generates a sense of vitality and serves as a proven treatment for Seasonal Affective Disorder (SAD). A computerized system controls selected portions of the lighting design, emulating daytime and nighttime.

The project's major challenges include designing an exterior wall system to withstand arctic temperature ranges from 90 degrees Fahrenheit to minus 70 degrees Fahrenheit, a strict energy code and stringent seismic design requirements. The exterior envelope establishes a composite 18-inch wall system that is thermally separated from the main structure. The building hosts a structural steel frame braced to resist seismic forces.

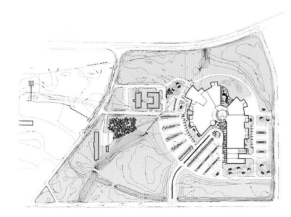

UNIVERSITY HOSPITALS AHUJA
MEDICAL CENTER

Design/Completion:	2010
Location:	Beachwood, Ohio
Client:	University Hospital
Size:	425,000 square feet
Association:	ARRAY Healthcare Facilities Solutions

The first-phase 144-bed acute-care hospital and integrated medical office building, located along a freeway in a suburb of Cleveland, is designed to connect with the community and its needs – from the exterior aesthetic reflecting the developing community surrounding it to the functional "community of care" promoting the welfare of both patients and staff.

The seven-story, curved patient tower is positioned to maximize the building's external visibility from the freeway and internal views to the adjoining wetlands, and to maintain those views in succeeding phases. Within the nursing unit, the curved plan enhances patient care and staff efficiency by minimizing staff travel, improving circulation of supplies, minimizing transport of patients, and maximizing opportunities for access to daylight and views. The terracotta-clad exterior reinterprets the materiality of the industrial brick buildings of the region in a new and contemporary way.

The planned three-phase medical campus is designed to function efficiently in its initial phase while providing a chassis for incremental growth into a 600-bed facility. The strategy for growth allows the public and service spines to expand incrementally in function and capacity as the needs of the facility evolve with minimal disruption to existing operations and while maintaining design integrity as expansion occurs.

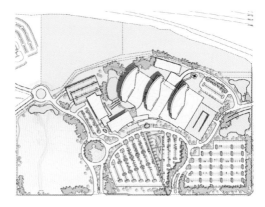

west elevation

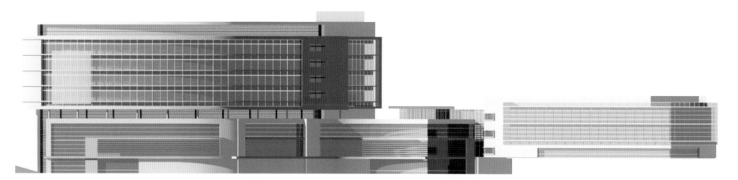

north elevation

KARBALA TEACHING HOSPITAL

Design/Completion:	2008
Location:	Karbala, Iraq
Client:	Ministry of Health
Size:	1 million square feet

The Karbala Teaching Hospital responds to the fundamental essence of the city itself, marking the destination point to a "journey of healing." The design and layout of the site, buildings and exterior take their cue from the fabric of the city streets, growing and forming around an enclosed garden that embodies a calming and enlightening environment.

The building façade is formed from a structural masonry skin that wraps the buildings to create a unique pattern, responding both to the local climate and internal functions. The pattern stems from a study of the city streets and geometric tesselations prominent in the region.

The 400-bed teaching hospital provides a comprehensive level of care including an emergency department with associated imaging, specialized women's services, surgery and outpatient clinics. The hospital also features on-site doctors' residences and extensive training facilities. Terraced underground parking and clear access points minimize patient and visitor travel distances while allowing for a natural landscaped site and maximized patient views from the bed towers. The hospital design is intended to become a prototype for the region – allowing for a flexible floor plate that can be adjusted to maximize or minimize the number of beds or patient care units required.

Main Design Drivers

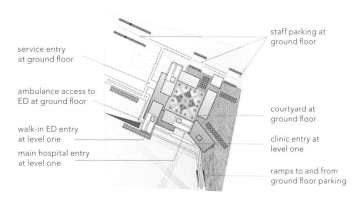

service entry
at ground floor

ambulance access to
ED at ground floor

walk-in ED entry
at level one

main hospital entry
at level one

staff parking at
ground floor

courtyard at
ground floor

clinic entry at
level one

ramps to and from
ground floor parking

FEDERAL UNIVERSITY
OF HEALTH SCIENCES

Design/Completion:	2008
Location:	Islamabad, Pakistan
Client:	Federal University of Health Sciences/Partners Harvard
	Medical International
Size:	700,000 square feet

The proposed facility design is inspired by Pakistani Urdu calligraphy, known as Nastaleeq. The design reflects the concept of the Urdu abstract letter, which is extended to all of the building exteriors.

Urdu calligraphy is designed into the many perforated walls, to embellish the building's exterior. The resultant texture and shadows are fascinating to see in the various illumination intensities throughout the day, evening and especially at night – when lighting from ground-level flood lamps highlight the walls.

An additional imperative is to supply an efficient circulation system and manage accessible patient and staff passage between the hospital's three towers via the enclosed connecting corridors.

Atrium spaces on the rooftops of the patient towers correspond to the Islamic traditional arch space concept, while offering a healthy outdoor environment for patients. A square plaza and several small courtyards provide a healing outdoor environment beneficial for patients' mental and physical health by applying Pakistani traditional architecture.

The shallow reflecting pool in the center of the plaza cools afternoon heat and adds much-needed humidity to the space. Continuing the Urdu theme, the semi-covered roof filters the harsh sun in summer while displaying a delightful pattern of shadows on the plaza's tiled flooring. The project includes a 150,000-square-foot medical school and research center.

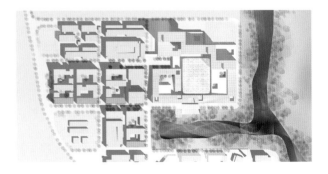

DANAT AL EMARAT WOMEN'S AND CHILDREN'S HOSPITAL

Design/Completion:	2011
Location:	Abu Dhabi, United Arab Emirates
Client:	United Eastern Medical Services
Size:	671,000 square feet

Danat Al Emarat Women's and Children's Hospital is a tribute to mothers, women and children. The tower is inspired by the fluid feminine forms of a graceful, flowing veil; mothers; water; and sand sculpted by the wind. The 21-story women's and children's hospital blends modern medicine with spaces that nurture the whole person focusing on body, mind and spirit.

The health center offers the latest technology, supporting the most advanced surgical and diagnostic procedures while the wellness center invites guests to a rejuvenating spa retreat. Diagnostic, treatment and clinic spaces continue the holistic experience.

Patient rooms could be easily mistaken as luxurious rooms found in any five-star hotel in Abu Dhabi. The mother's room is an embracing oval womb shape that nurtures, protects and honors mother and baby with healing views, 6-foot-long closets and a family seating area that encircles the patient for comfort and care.

The world-class hospital will be a memorable and meaningful landmark that serves as a destination of excellence for women and children not only in the Middle East, but throughout the world.

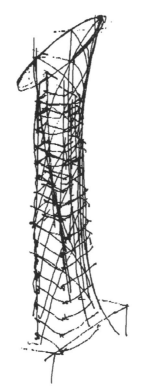
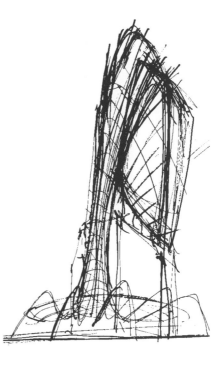

AMERICAN BRITISH COWDRAY CANCER CENTER

Design/Completion: 2009

Location: Mexico City, Mexico

Client: American British Cowdray

Size: 65,000 square feet

The synergy of the American British Cowdray Cancer Center creates an optimal treatment environment for patients challenged with persevering through an intimidating and life-changing experience.

Located in Mexico City, this comprehensive oncology center integrates radiation therapy, chemotherapy, minor procedures, clinical multi-specialty teams, diagnostics as well as patient support and education. Many of the services currently scattered throughout the campus are now consolidated into one multi-modality center. This facility also brings together many oncology specialists in one building, creating a multi-disciplined team organization for physicians and staff.

Chemotherapy is located on the top floor and provides views of the city skyline through landscaped terraces just outside the windows. A healing garden, which provides respite for patients, visitors and staff, is adjacent to Christian and Jewish chapels.

A portion of the project site is allotted for a neighborhood park to further serve the community and integrate the building into the neighborhood fabric. The entire street edge of the building has landscaping along the perimeter. Patient drop-off and valet services are available at two levels, and grade-level parking is located immediately adjacent to the building.

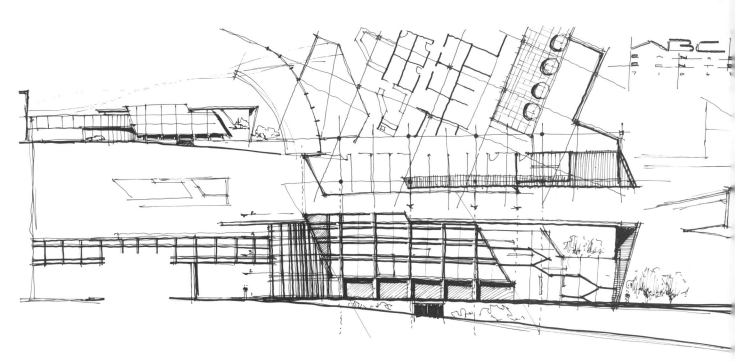

ENZE MEDICAL CENTER

Design/Completion:	2006
Location:	Taizhou, Zhejiang Province, P.R. China
Client:	Taizhou Hospital
Size:	1.6 million square feet

Located in a developing part of China, the design for a new greenfield tertiary hospital emphasizes state-of-the-art care, responding to the needs of a growing community while protecting the region's limited resources through sustainable design.

In Chinese, the Yuan is a circular shape that symbolizes wholeness, perfection and harmony between people and Mother Nature. The Yuan is used to embrace the campus, defining key elements and zones of care and allowing the symbol of the circle to be both literally and figuratively expressed throughout the design.

Unity, bridging the past to the future in a facility that is one with its community, is the concept for this 1,500-bed wellness hospital and campus. The unity concept is the foundation of the design's four guiding principles: healing environments, sustainability, connectivity and disaster response.

Simple yet elegant, the Yuan unifies and creates an integrated environment that delivers the best in healthcare. The result is a design that establishes a new, vibrant healthcare community within a growing population.

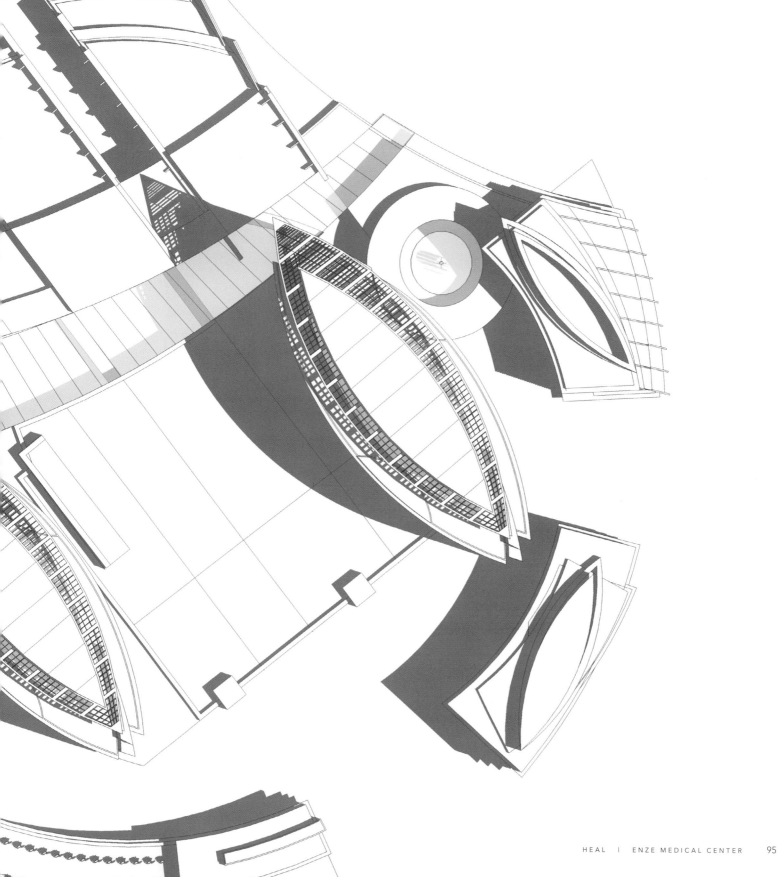

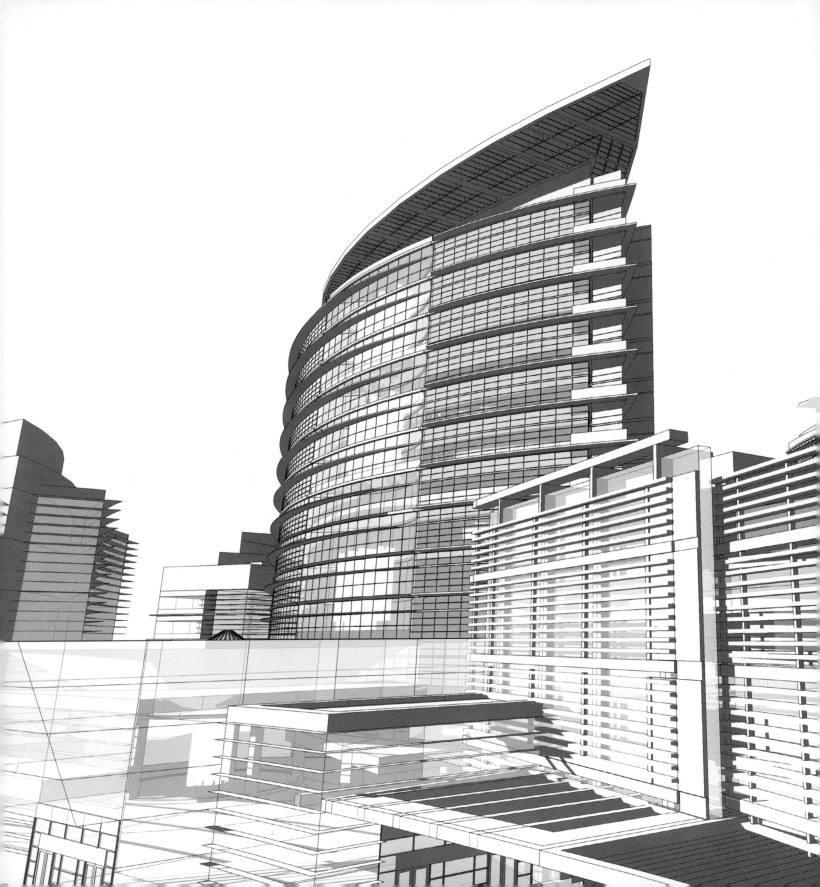

ABBOTT NORTHWESTERN HEART HOSPITAL

Design/Completion: 2005

Location: Minneapolis, Minnesota

Client: Abbott Northwestern Hospital

Size: 225,000 square feet

The renowned cardiovascular services of Abbott Northwestern Hospital and the Minneapolis Heart Institute joined together to develop Abbott Northwestern Heart Hospital. The 128-bed heart hospital anchors the existing campus while serving patients and their families from across the upper Midwest.

The eight-story addition provides a progressive and timeless image for the main campus while relating to the scale of the surrounding community. Brick, stone and metal panel colors tie visually to the original building but in a more contemporary architectural expression.

The two-story lobby, with its stone water feature and large expanses of windows, improves wayfinding and reduces initial stress on patients and their families. A dynamic rotunda encircles an existing elevator while transitioning visitors from the parking garage into the lobby.

The facility is designed as a place to treat the whole person – mind, body and spirit – that blends the best of modern medicine's complementary techniques. Patients benefit from technological advances, a healing environment and a program of integrative therapies including therapeutic massage, music therapy and guided imagery. Patient care areas are designed to improve the patient experience and improve staff efficiency and satisfaction. The hospital is designed with spaces for education, conferencing, relaxation and renewal for the staff.

CHRISTUS MUGUERZA TUXTLA HOSPITAL

Design/Completion:	2007
Location:	Tuxtla Gutiérrez, Chiapas, Mexico
Client:	Grupo Christus Muguerza
Size:	93,000 square feet

The Christus Muguerza Tuxtla Hospital will offer an expanded range of health services to the community following the completion of a major renovation and addition. When completed, the hospital will offer the community access to emergency, radiology and surgery services.

The project innovatively integrates an existing 1960s hotel with an acute care addition, both aesthetically and functionally. The hotel will be converted into overnight patient rooms, administrative, kitchen/dining, support areas and medical office space. The urban site – along Belisario Domínguez Boulevard – provides a street view for the new hospital, while diagnostic and treatment functions are located on the east side of the building.

The main entrance, located internally from the central site access, leads to a welcoming atrium space with elevators and connections into the renovated hotel. The exterior motif features brightly colored mosaic panels and architectural mesh, celebrating the typical Zoque ethnic group ribbon costumes and pottery indigenous to the area. Large expanses of glass wall were used to create a theme uniting the two building portions.

AL QUDRA HEALTHCARE MEDICAL CAMPUS

Design/Completion:	2014
Location:	Abu Dhabi, United Arab Emirates
Client:	Al Qudra Health Care L.L.C
Size:	4.6 million square feet

Concentric rings growing outward as a finger touches the water symbolize the radiating influence and impact of the world-class Al Qudra Children's Hospital and Medical Campus upon the city, the UAE and the world.

Starting at the center of the site around an interactive reflecting pool, the campus grows outward in a radial pattern. The integration of water and its interaction with the buildings provides an ever-changing feature in light, sound and reflection.

Perpetual motion – a symbol of healthy, happy children – informs the design of the buildings to create a child-friendly campus. This idea is reflected in the creation of dynamic form, flowing lines and playful textures.

Phase one is dedicated to the establishment of a comprehensive children's hospital, ambulatory surgery center, primary care clinic, hotel and residences.

The client and design team's desire was to create a sustainable building that would respond to the outside environment in a number of different ways. Photovoltaic roof screens and building skin harness the sun's energy to provide alternative energy. A double-skin system assists in solar heat gain while allowing for moderated air temperature. Cantilevered floor slabs extend beyond the building skin to provide shading. Rooftop screens shade mechanical equipment and building façades while providing shade for rooftop gardens and open courtyards below.

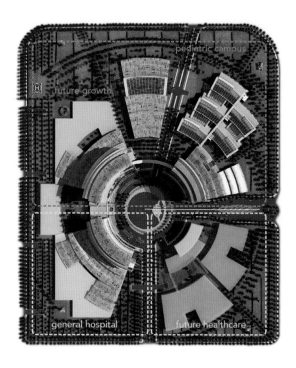

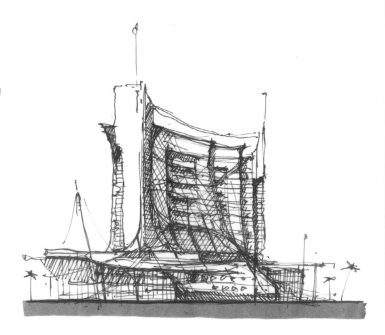

ren's Hospital

ROYAL CHILDREN'S HOSPITAL

Design/Completion: 2011

Location: Melbourne, Victoria, Australia

Client: Royal Children's Hospital; State Government of Victoria, Australia;
Department of Human Services

Size: 1.6 million square feet

Association: Billard Leese and Bates Smart

Royal Children's Hospital is designed to be a world-class facility, offering the latest in quality care in a healing environment that is responsive to the needs of children, their families and staff. Interactive playgrounds, a two-story coral reef aquarium, a Scienceworks wonders of science display, a bean bag theater showing the latest movies and a star-gazing Starlight Room are a few of the unique positive distractions for kids.

The children's hospital is based on family-centered care. More than 85 percent of the rooms will be single-bed rooms, providing privacy for patients and their families. Rooms will be designed to feel more like home with a place to put personal belongings, state-of-the-art entertainment systems and lighting controls. Storage areas and stay-over areas are also designed for family members.

Gathering areas and outdoor balconies, which serve as retreats, are on each floor. In addition, the new hospital will house a supermarket and a gymnasium. A new Family Resource Center is located nearby to support families with private cubicles, laundry areas, a lounge and kitchen, personal care suites and an outside courtyard.

The new hospital, designed to be Australia's first five-star Green Star hospital, will be friendly to the environment – reducing water and energy consumption as well as greenhouse gas emissions.

SALEM HOSPITAL REGIONAL HEALTH SERVICES

Design/Completion:	2009
Location:	Salem, Oregon
Client:	Salem Hospital
Size:	347,000 square feet

Salem Hospital's patient tower addition beautifully integrates the existing buildings while creating a progressive new campus gateway. The design and construction team provided an integrated three-phase approach to project delivery including programming, design and construction.

A primary focus of the campus design is to improve way-finding and reduce pedestrian/vehicular conflicts. The new addition accomplishes this by creating a grand entry drive punctuated by the new tower and complementary reflecting gardens with local stone and plant material.

The tower location is based upon critical adjacencies, connectivity to the existing buildings and site constraints due to boundaries and waterways. The building unifies the campus while improving the image and providing a stress-reducing main lobby, concourse, café and series of public and staff bridges.

The facility provides critical expanded services such as a replacement for the emergency department, interventional services, imaging services, critical care and acute care beds in flexible 30-bed floors that are expandable to 90 beds in the future. Private, acuity-adaptable patient rooms welcome family members and provide garden views and vistas to the surrounding community. The interior reflects the colors and materials of the region focusing on warm day-lighting and access to nature.

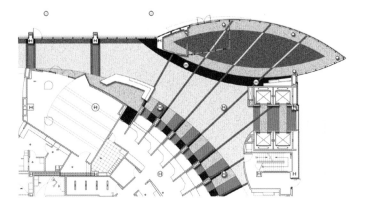

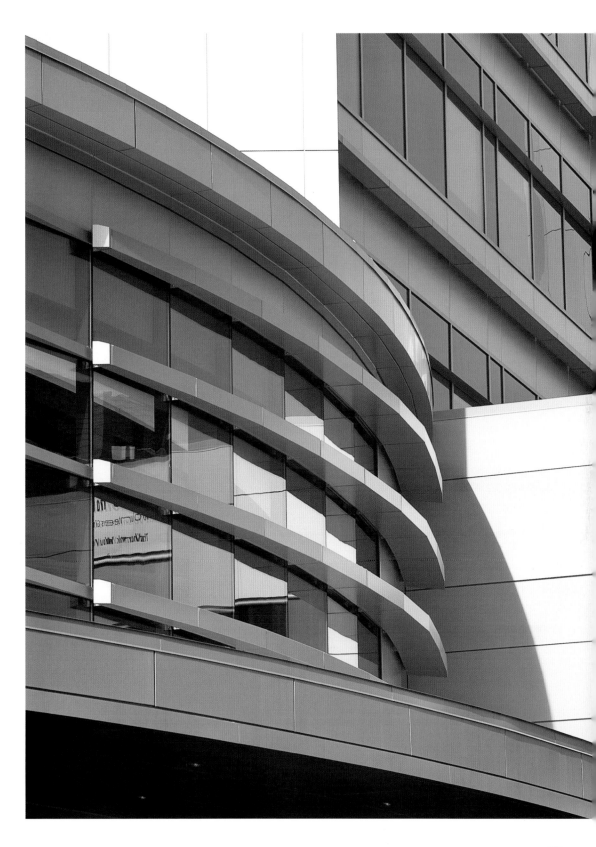

LYNN CANCER INSTITUTE – HARVEY & PHYLLIS SANDLER PAVILION

Design/Completion: 2008
Location: Boca Raton, Florida
Client: Boca Raton Community Hospital
Size: 100,000 square feet

The Boca Raton Cancer Institute is designed to express competence and instill comfort in patients who are in need of hope. Making the cancer center a healthcare destination, enhancing the patient and family experience and providing clinical excellence and patient safety are the center's guiding design principles.

One of Florida's top cancer centers, the institute offers multimodality care, which brings the entire medical team to each patient in one location. The comprehensive cancer care center contains a radiation oncology and imaging center, hematology/oncology clinic and chemotherapy and infusion center. Reflective of the nearby coastal beaches, the center is designed with bright, clean accent colors with a warm, neutral background palette.

The three-story, naturally lit main atrium serves as a beacon of hope, uplifting patients' spirits as they enter the building. Patient treatment spaces include family members as a part of the care-giving team. The infusion therapy area, surrounded by large expanses of glass with views to nature, incorporates private treatment areas for quiet conversations with family members as well as open spaces for group interaction. Private gardens provide therapeutic areas allowing reflection and contemplation.

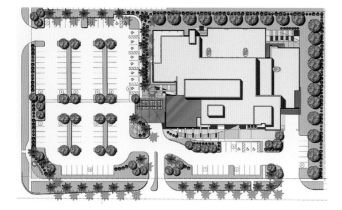

PHOENIX CHILDREN'S HOSPITAL

Design/Completion:	2010
Location:	Phoenix, Arizona
Client:	Phoenix Children's Hospital
Size:	776,000 square feet

The patient care tower addition for Phoenix Children's Hospital highlights a playfully sophisticated design that respects existing aesthetics while strengthening the Children's brand. The campus creates a healing oasis within the desert surroundings while the tower becomes the blooming desert flower that transforms in appearance from day to night.

Flowing curved forms, bold geometric blocks of color and incredible views from within transform the pediatric patient experience to support the hospital's mission of treating the entire family. The curvilinear tower is divided into three parts to reduce the impact of its scale.

The entry court is punctuated by a large vertical sail. The three-story atrium welcomes patients and families with shaded transparency and the colorfully animated interiors within. The southern exposure is capped by a cantilevered parapet on the southeast end reaching boldly out to the community with a purple glow of hope.

Care has been taken to improve the family journey through lush and whimsical landscaping accentuated with colorful sculpture and soothing water features. The facility utilizes indigenous color, playful animal sculptures and desert flowers to visually organize each floor. Strategic day-lighting offers a sense of calm in major spaces, punctuates corridors and creates striking vistas within patient rooms. Places of escape integrate the indoors and outdoors, providing families choices and control over the daily milieu.

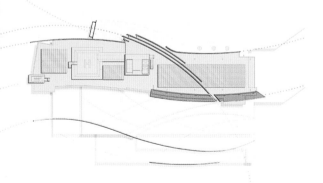

HEAL | PHOENIX CHILDREN'S HOSPITAL 125

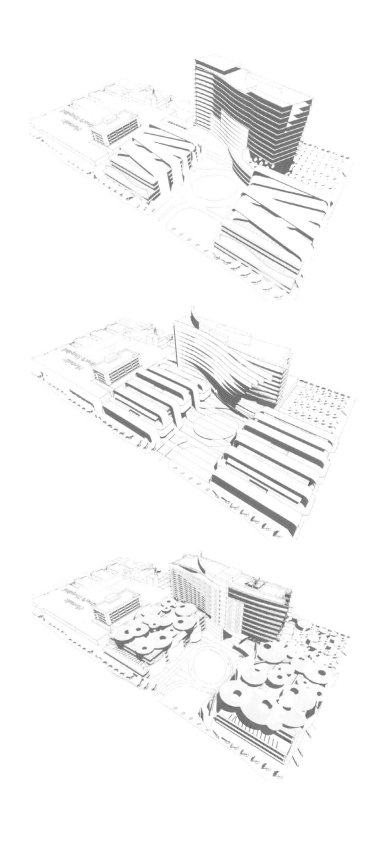

KING HUSSEIN CANCER CENTER

Design/Completion:	2011
Location:	Amman, Jordan
Client:	King Hussein Cancer Center
Size:	440,000 square feet
Association:	SIGMA – Consulting Engineers

The 440,000-square-foot King Hussein Cancer Center will be the premier cancer research and treatment center for Jordan and surrounding countries in the Middle East region.

Like the city, the design of the building is progressive and modern, yet steeped in tradition, respecting its historic past. Reflecting the landscape of the ancient city with its intertwining design, the building façade to the south and east features punctuated fenestration patterns and stepped elements that mimic the hills in the distance. This design lessens the impact of the 14-story vertical tower in the urban area.

A glass tower, the building's tallest element, can be viewed from major intersections, which converge in the area. The Jerusalem stone engages with the glass – as if protecting and highlighting a jewel. Public areas of the building, such as the bridge, atrium and family lounges, are exposed with glass promoting openness in contrast to the solidity of the stone. The faceted glass is transparent during the day and night, openly displaying the lifesaving activities occurring within the building.

The comprehensive cancer center will feature 152 adult and pediatric inpatient rooms, extensive diagnostic and treatment facilities and outpatient clinics. The design will implement best practices and benchmarks from top cancer centers across the United States, and will follow design guidelines set by the American Institute of Architects for Design and Construction of Health Care Facilities and the Joint Commission International Standards for Accreditation. The cancer center will offer the most advanced cancer technology available to date. It is envisioned to be a healing environment for the mind, body and spirit addressing the full range of medical, psychological and social issues associated with cancer care.

DUBAI CANCER CENTER

Design/Completion: 2009

Location: Dubai, United Arab Emirates

Client: confidential

Size: 425,000 square feet

HKS recently completed a design study for a potential cancer center client in Dubai. The study focused on a potential design solution for a new, free-standing, comprehensive cancer center blending cutting edge technology with patient-centered care. The cancer hospital is envisioned to be a "beacon of healthcare" to guide patients in navigating their challenging journey through cancer healing with confidence and hope.

Inspired by the rich history of Dubai, the design concept's modern, evocative building forms relate to the vibrant urban context and recall Dubai's unique heritage. The hospital's sail-like form extends an invitation to the people of Dubai, the United Arab Emirates and their world neighbors to experience the healing within. The multi-layered dynamic forms reflect the essential need for a connection to daily life, the community, region and world around. Water surrounds the building forms while the tower meets the earth in a gentle embrace honoring all who enter this protected realm of healing. A bridge extends as an invitation to initiate the processional pathway to healing, welcoming patients and their families with gracious hospitality and dignity.

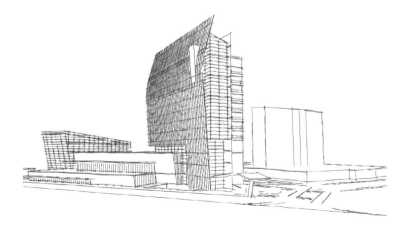

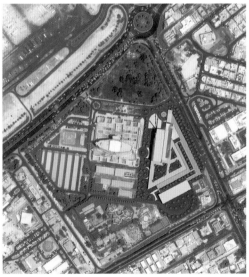

NORTHERN BATCH HOPE HOSPITAL

Design/Completion:	1997
Location:	Salford, England
Client:	Salford Royal Hospitals NHS Trust
Size:	500,000 square feet
Association:	under the auspices of RyderHKS International

Salford Royal Hospitals NHS Trust's $227-million development allows the integration of new outpatient facilities and inpatient beds with the hospital's existing diagnostic and treatment hub. More than 410 new beds are housed in the new addition – allowing 850 patient beds in total. The project also includes the construction of full emergency and women's services facilities.

The new addition and renovations reconfigure the site, promoting clarity and ease of use. The siting of the hospital creates a new civic face for the city of Salford. In addition, the entrance is connected to public spaces that are linked to department reception and waiting areas – promoting easy wayfinding for staff, patients and visitors.

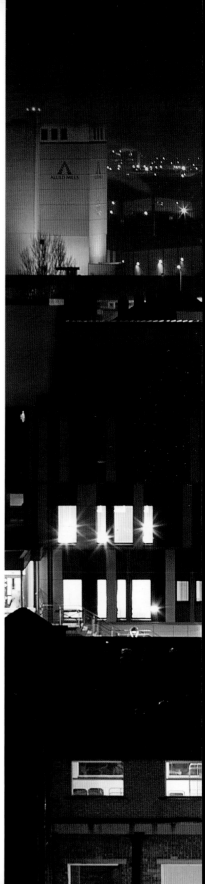

3 | REST

W Dallas - Victory Hotel & Residences   140

Montage Beverly Hills   144

Shutters on the Beach   146

Montage Laguna Beach   148

Capella Pedregal   152

Four Seasons Hualalai   154

Tucker's Point Club   158

Jean-Michel Cousteau Fiji Islands Resort   160

Las Ventanas al Paraíso   162

Four Seasons Resort at Sharm el-Sheikh   166

The Ritz-Carlton, Half Moon Bay   170

The Westin Kierland Resort and Spa   172

Hyatt Regency Tamaya   174

The Ritz-Carlton, Bachelor Gulch   176

Suncadia Lodge   180

Four Seasons Scottsdale at Troon North   184

The Venetian Macao-Resort-Hotel   190

Atlantis Phase II   192

Loews Ventana Canyon Resort   194

Hilton Orlando Convention Center Hotel   196

JW Marriott San Antonio   198

Hyatt Lost Pines Resort and Spa   200

W DALLAS - VICTORY HOTEL & RESIDENCES

Design/Completion:	2006
Location:	Dallas, Texas
Client:	Hillwood Development, Gatehouse Capital
Size:	900,000 square feet

From its cowboy-cool living room that boasts a glowing glass wall to its glass-floor Ghostbar balcony, the W offers its guests a unique and memorable experience from start to finish.

The 252-room, hip hotel offers energetic ambience including a vibrant living room lobby and a signature restaurant. Rising above the hotel's top floors, to the north and south, are 150 luxury condominiums.

The W tower participates in the energy and environment of Victory Plaza's Times Square concept as a focal point and as an overlook to the space. The project is a series of lifestyle experiences as one moves vertically through the tower from street-life entertainment to an infinity-edge pool, residences and Ghostbar in the sky.

Metaphorically, the W tower serves as the campanile or bell tower to Victory's public plaza. Positioned at the southern edge of Victory Plaza, the tower evokes a modern, progressive expression that reshapes the Dallas skyline.

It speaks to the future of Dallas with modern, progressive architecture, which is in contrast to many of the existing downtown buildings. Its cantilevered projecting wing allows the building to poetically meet the sky. The hotel, with its sweeping glass curves, speaks of attitude, sophistication and style.

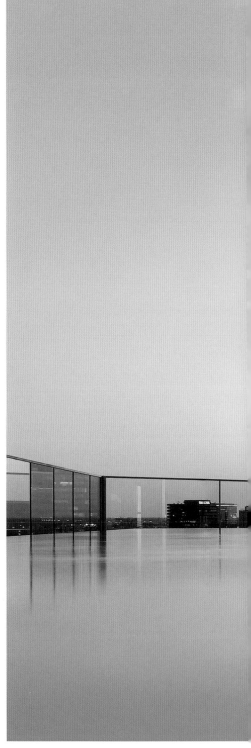

MONTAGE BEVERLY HILLS

Design/Completion:	2008
Location:	Los Angeles, California
Client:	Montage Beverly Hills
Size:	422,000 square feet

Montage Beverly Hills is a unique urban lifestyle hotel that pays homage to the Golden Age of Hollywood in a modern-day luxury setting.

Located between Canon and Beverly Drives in the city's Golden Triangle district, the five-star hotel revitalizes a 2.5-acre abandoned retail site one block from the posh retailers of Rodeo Drive. HKS Hill Glazier Studio worked side-by-side with the mayor, city council and neighborhood groups throughout the design, development and construction process, and even set up a project hotline for citizens. The resulting urban jewel is a modern yet timeless re-interpretation of Hollywood glamour. It is also one of only four hotels worldwide to earn LEED Gold certification and the first project of its kind to be LEED certified.

The design intent was to evoke a timeless elegance, capturing the sophisticated residential character of southern California's glamorous estates of the 1920s and 1930s. Inspired by the Spanish Colonial Revival roots and Mediterranean architecture that are part of the area's history, the hotel's exterior features Spanish style arches, plaster wall surfaces and terracotta tile roofs with authentic tile detailing. Montage also boasts a 30,000-square-foot courtyard garden – the first public green space in the Golden Triangle.

SHUTTERS ON THE BEACH

Design/Completion:	1993
Location:	Santa Monica, California
Client:	E.T. Whitehall Santa Monica Partners L.P.
Size:	210,000 square feet

Long considered the quintessential California beach resort, Shutters on the Beach is reminiscent of the traditional architecture of America's historic seaside resorts and the inviting, turn-of-the-century, Craftsman-style cottages of the southern California coast.

The hotel is comprised of three separate buildings, all visually connected by intricately detailed slate-gray shingled siding, flower-covered trellises, balconies and cabana-striped awnings. The tallest buildings contain the sun-drenched pool deck; the front of the 200-room resort opens onto the famous Santa Monica beach promenade.

While all the buildings feature shutters, broad eaves and brackets, each has its own unique character inside. Throughout the public areas and in each of the guestrooms, elements such as shutters, white-washed paneled walls and French doors with terraces embrace the resort's informal beach theme.

The warm and inviting lobby offers two large fireplaces, intimate conversation areas and a substantial balcony overlooking the ocean. Throughout the hotel, original artwork, lithographs and striking objects d'art add charm, elegance and style.

MONTAGE LAGUNA BEACH

Design/Completion:	2003
Location:	Laguna Beach, California
Client:	The Athens Group, Montage Hotels & Resorts
Size:	453,000 square feet

Situated on a 30-acre oceanfront bluff with breathtaking panoramas of the Pacific Ocean and stunning Craftsman-style architecture, the award-winning Montage Laguna Beach has become the standard for casual elegance, luxury lifestyle design and signature service.

Located in the picturesque artists' colony of Laguna Beach between Los Angeles and San Diego, Montage's definitive architectural design dates to Laguna's artistic roots of the early 1900s, when the California Arts & Crafts movement was in full swing. Distinctive period design elements define the luxury beach resort including classic wood and stone architecture, crown moldings, rich dark wood, copper gutters and shingle-style roofs.

Montage's 250 spacious guestrooms, including 37 beach bungalow-style rooms, and public areas are sumptuously decorated in a sophisticated yet comfortable turn-of-the-century style, with dark wood furnishings, muted color schemes and authentic artwork by celebrated California artists. Each room has a private oceanfront balcony with a spectacular view of the Laguna Beach coastline.

CAPELLA PEDREGAL

Design/Completion:	2009
Location:	Cabo San Lucas, Baja California Sur, Mexico
Client:	CP Trust c/o Hotel Ventures International, LLC
Size:	521,000 square feet

Nestled on the Baja peninsula between the Pacific Ocean and the Sea of Cortez, Capella Pedregal fronts the ocean and is built into a backdrop of rugged mountains, blanketed with the exotic vegetation of the Sonoran Desert.

The 66-room, all-suite hotel offers guests intimacy and serenity. Guestrooms open to an ocean-view terrace or balcony and boast private plunge pools. Original materials and local craftsmanship create authentic, simple and honest living spaces.

The restaurant allows guests to taste the essence of fine Mexican cuisine. A stunning infinity-edge pool and sun deck link the hotel and the private residence club while providing shaded areas for conversations.

Private residence club units, known as Las Residencias, include 13 three-bedroom and 18 four-bedroom units. Unit sizes range from 3,500 to 4,500 square feet. Patios and balconies open to personal plunge pools and striking ocean views. A grotto-style pool cascades from multiple levels down to the beach.

The 18 residences, called Las Casonas, are the ultimate in luxury living. Units are available in three or four bedrooms and range from 5,000 to 7,000 square feet. Each home hosts its own private pool and a variety of marina and ocean views. With a separate gated entrance, Las Casonas offers residents full privacy.

FOUR SEASONS HUALALAI

Design/Completion: 1996
Location: Ka'upulehu Kona, Hawaii
Client: Hualalai Development Corp.
Size: 265,000 square feet

The Four Seasons Resort Hualalai was designed to enhance and celebrate the natural beauty and climate of the Hawaiian Islands. Inspired by the architecture of traditional Hawaiian villages, the resort fulfills the concept of Kipuka – a lushly landscaped paradise surrounded by molten lava flows.

The resort comprises 246 expansive bungalow-style guest rooms, including 31 suites housed in a series of individual villa buildings. Guestrooms are organized around four informal courtyards, each with its own distinct and unique character. All guestrooms feature ocean views, private terraces, open-air bathrooms and traditional Hawaiian furnishings. Guest suites are designed to blur the distinction between indoor and outdoor space, with an elaborate system of sliding pocket doors and shutters providing the ability to completely open up many exterior walls.

The main resort amenities and back-of-house support areas are decentralized, reinforcing a more residential scale and reducing the apparent size of the project. The lobby, restaurants, meeting spaces and spa are designed as separate open-air pavilions – many with unobstructed views of the Pacific Ocean. The golf clubhouse is also located in a separate facility and sited to allow for views to the 18th fairway of the Jack Nicklaus signature golf course.

TUCKER'S POINT CLUB

Design/Completion:	2009
Location:	Tucker's Town, Bermuda
Client:	Tucker's Point Club
Size:	173,000 square feet

Dramatically perched above Castle Harbour's electric blue waters, Tucker's Point Hotel and Spa sits as the crown jewel of the Tucker's Point Club development. This Bermudian-style hotel provides comfort and luxury while maintaining classic British Colonial influences.

Fifty-two of the 88 ultra-luxury rooms are in the stately Manor House, which sits as a backdrop to the lobby and is the spotlight of the resort. The remaining rooms are nestled in three buildings sitting below the Manor House, capturing a hillside village experience that creates the uniqueness and character of the resort. All guestrooms include expansive terraces offering breathtaking views.

The back views of the property are as commanding as the front. A palm allee defines the space, with a croquet lawn and a dramatic infinity-edge pool overlooking a lush grotto at one end and the waters of Harrington Sound at the other. The spa provides an outdoor garden, relaxation courtyards as well as a Yoga and Tai Chi lawn, while the conference center engages the outside space for large group functions.

The Point Restaurant, with its English-style long bar and outdoor terrace, celebrates outdoor space above all. Elevated above the pool, dramatic views here are magnified with memorable sunsets and warm nights on the twin fireplace terrace.

JEAN-MICHEL COUSTEAU FIJI ISLANDS RESORT

Design/Completion:	2005
Location:	Vanua Levu, Fiji Islands
Client:	Coastal Inns "Fiji" Ltd., Jean-Michel Cousteau Fiji Resort
Size:	7,500 square feet

At the Jean-Michel Cousteau Fiji Islands Resort, guests are immersed in the true nature of Fiji, while staying in comfort and style. The resort's quest for customer satisfaction is further defined with the addition of the Point Reef Villas.

The award-winning, five-star resort is one of the most renowned vacation destinations in the South Pacific. Located on the island of Vanua Levu on 17 acres of a coconut plantation, the accommodations overlook the peaceful waters of Savusavu Bay.

The luxurious and private villas feature the best of resort living and accommodations. Redefining the boundaries of indoor and outdoor living, the gracious villa combines contemporary style and natural elegance with traditional Fijian architecture and ambience. The result is villa design incorporating the finest of materials, amenities and views of the sea.

Villa guests approach along a curving stone pathway, surrounded by organic privacy walls and landscaped with lush foliage and tropical flowers. Once inside, the guest is greeted with layered experiences of indoor foliage, rocks, sun decks, a private infinity-edge pool and views of the Fijian aqua blue ocean.

LAS VENTANAS AL PARAÍSO

Design/Completion:	1997
Location:	Los Cabos, Mexico
Client:	Javier Burillo
Size:	288,000 square feet

The desert oasis feel of this luxury resort and spa was influenced by the Baja Peninsula's temperate climate and indigenous plant life. The resort includes 61 guest suites, 36 king rooms, 20 double rooms and four superior suites.

All are situated in low-rise buildings connected by stairs, bridges and curving paths dotted with desert flowers and palm trees. The white stucco walls of the resort convey the coolness and relaxed comfort of the sea. The design of each upstairs suite includes balconies that look over the Sea of Cortez and contain telescopes for stargazing and whale watching. Local artisans and workers were employed for the construction and craftsmanship of the resort. The lobby is open and provides pedestrian circulation to different areas of the resort. The thatched-roof lobby looks out onto the ocean, while open walkways are covered with latilla. The intricate network of swimming pools leads to swim-up bars and an outdoor grill.

Another dining option is the Wine Room, surrounding guests with over 2,400 bottles of wine. There is a full service hotel spa available to guests. The resort offers a conference center and is equipped to outfit visitors with any business need.

FOUR SEASONS RESORT AT SHARM EL-SHEIKH

Design/Completion:	2002
Location:	Sinai Peninsula, Egypt
Client:	Alexandria Co. for Real Estate
Size:	185,000 square feet

The Four Seasons Resort at Sharm el-Sheikh is located on the southernmost point of the Sinai Peninsula and inspired by the traditional hillside towns of the Mediterranean and Middle East. Rendered in an Islamic architectural vernacular, guests arrive beneath a canopy of date palms in a "citadel" structure that contains the lobby, main restaurants and meeting space.

Located at the top of this steeply sloped site, these public areas command dramatic views of the Red Sea. The tiers of guest rooms and resort amenities follow the steeply sloping site down to the water's edge. The use of domes, simplified Islamic arches that evoke traditional forms, parapet crenellations and roof gardens are reminiscent of this romantic style. Deep overhangs over luxurious exterior balconies respond to the harsh climate while keeping interiors cool and private.

Courtyards cooled by fountains and shaded by canopies of tall palms provide gateways to the various guestrooms – all of which have ocean views. Even standard guest rooms are designed as small suites with separate bedroom and parlor spaces, large terraced exterior living areas and natural light-filled bathrooms. Fabrics and furnishings are simple, reflecting the sophisticated yet casual vernacular of this coastal region.

THE RITZ-CARLTON, HALF MOON BAY

Design/Completion:	2001
Location:	Half Moon Bay, California
Client:	The Athens Group
Size:	298,000 square feet

Nestled in a remote part of Northern California along the rugged cliff edges of the Pacific Ocean, The Ritz-Carlton, Half Moon Bay was conceived as a grand seaside resort in the spirit of Newport and Rhode Island's spectacular residences. This luxury golf resort was built into the sloping bluff to fully utilize the natural terrain and take complete advantage of the ocean and shoreline panoramas.

The 261 hotel rooms sit on 14 windswept acres and are distributed between the Main Lodge and individual two-story bungalows. The picturesque landscape with rolling sea, jagged cliffs and pristine golf courses is reminiscent of iconic seaside golf resorts throughout the British Isles. Shingle-style architecture was the logical choice to evoke both the historic references and climatic conditions.

The floor divisions are expressed on the hotel's exterior through the use of rusticated stone, balconies, columns and varied window groupings. Chimneys, gables and shed-style dormers punctuate the roofline, adding 19th century-inspired flair.

The colors of its façade – steel gray on foggy days, golden-hued on sunny ones – reflect the moods of the sea and sky. The hotel's nautical theme reaches a crescendo in the boat-like Navio restaurant, with its spectacular barrel-vaulted ceiling.

THE WESTIN KIERLAND RESORT AND SPA

Design/Completion:	2002
Location:	Phoenix, Arizona
Client:	Woodbine Southwest Corporation
Size:	712,500 square feet

The Westin Kierland Resort and Spa's picturesque silhouette is inspired by the mountain ranges found throughout Arizona, including the Mogollon Rim, and those surrounding the site, such as Camelback Mountain and Pinnacle Peak. The highest point of the resort, the peaks of the twin towers, mark the entry to the hotel. From these peaks, the resort's massing steps down to one and two stories. This stepping is softened with roofs that mimic the dramatic massing of the Arizona mountain ranges.

The façade's color gradation, derived from local stone layers, is reminiscent of the stratified layers of rock exposed in many of the canyons north of the site. A deep terracotta color is found at the base of the resort to help anchor the building to the earth. Above the base, the color varies from the deep terracotta to a rich, brown sandstone to a pale limestone on the top floors.

Generous garden landscape foliage and shaded parking separate the resort from the perimeter streets. The rolling fairways and lakes of Kierland Golf Club form the northern and western boundaries of the resort site. A walking path with plant identification markers provides an interesting and scenic route from the resort to the golf clubhouse or the Kierland Commons specialty retail village.

HYATT REGENCY TAMAYA

Design/Completion:	2001
Location:	Santa Ana Pueblo, New Mexico
Client:	Santa Ana Pueblo; Santa Ana Hospitality Corp.; Southern Sandoval Investments, Ltd.; Santa Ana Golf Corp.
Size:	332,500 square feet

Located on the banks of the Rio Grande at the base of Sandia Peak, the Hyatt Regency Tamaya Resort is part of a new resort community at the Santa Ana Pueblo. The architecture of the resort is inspired by the historic adobe structures of the original Santa Ana Pueblo, which dates back to the early 17th century. Every effort has been made to respect and preserve the building traditions of pueblo architecture and the Native American people. The end result is a resort that is an integral part of the Tamaya community while featuring the amenities normally found in a luxury resort.

Authentic building materials, including stone, wood and adobe, convey a feeling of place to guests. The arrival court, framed by thick adobe walls and a deep portal, contains a mesquite-burning fireplace at the entrance. The guest rooms are located in two wings called Turquoise and Pumpkin, which refer to the two clans of the ancient Santa Ana Pueblo, and are a reminder of the ancient inhabitants of the historic land.

The overall design is based on a series of grids, giving an organic feel to the layout of the structures. This also gives the resort the appearance of having been built at different periods, a quality inherent to the design of the pueblos, which were built over several centuries. Special care was taken in the axial design so that all the rooms have views of the stunning natural landscape of Sandia Peak. Open-air courtyards promote a sense of intimacy with the surroundings of the river and mountains. Guests are able to learn more about the art and history of the Pueblo at Shipapuh, the Santa Ana Tribal Cultural Center Museum, which offers a cultural experience of the Native American way of life.

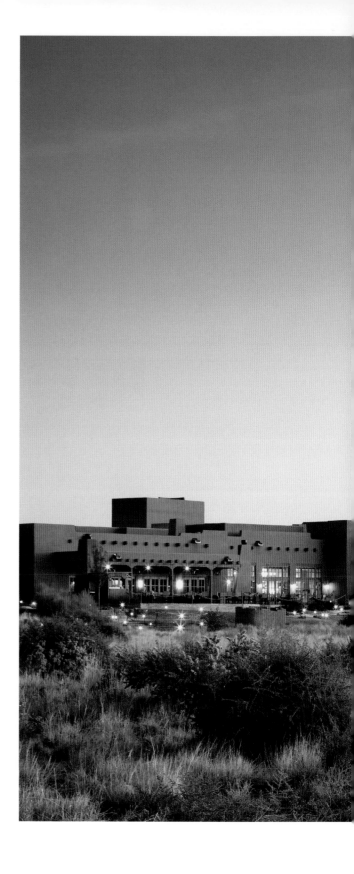

THE RITZ-CARLTON, BACHELOR GULCH

Design/Completion:	2002
Location:	Vail, Colorado
Client:	Vail Associates Inc., The Athens Group
Size:	450,000 square feet

The Ritz-Carlton, Bachelor Gulch is the premier luxury development in the Vail/Beaver Creek Resort area. The hotel is the centerpiece of the Mountain Center complex that houses ski and other recreational amenities at the mid-mountain base of the ski area and home sites.

With expansive views of the Vail Valley and the surrounding mountain ranges, the 237-room hotel complex includes 33 club-level luxury condominiums, a 21,000-square-foot spa with 19 treatment rooms, restaurants, meeting space and a 54-unit Ritz-Carlton Club comprised of two- and three-bedroom residential units.

The Ritz-Carlton, Bachelor Gulch is constructed with logs and moss rock, recalling the iconic architectural traditions of the grand National Park lodges of the Rocky Mountains. Design inspiration for the luxury hotel and club was taken from examples such as the Old Faithful Inn at Yellowstone. The rustic feel of an historic Grand Lodge is captured on the inside through the use of stone, logs and exposed timbers, while the outside features dormer windows, broad sweeping gables and log balconies. A stone and timber porte-cochère entry welcomes guests and protects them from inclement weather.

SUNCADIA LODGE

Design/Completion: 2008

Location: Roslyn, Washington

Client: Destination Development

Size: 380,000 square feet

Located in the Wenatchee National Forest in Washington State, Suncadia Lodge is respectful of the natural world around it. Set along the edge of the Cle Elum River Valley, the lodge is a contemporary adaptation of the west's National Parks. The buildings feature generous openings, light-colored timber brackets, terned metal roofs and large-scale board and batten siding.

Guests are drawn to the views of Mt. Baldy and Thomas Mountain through two-story glass windows. Timber grown locally from in-state resources, such as oak, pine and fir, is the primary building material. Passing through smaller rooms and corridors, guests will discover the dining room, which also shares the beamed ceilings, designed to maximize the view of the valley and mountains with views up and down the Cle Elum River.

Nestled between the hotel and village, the spa is placed into a mountain glade providing a mountain oasis sheltered from the wind and in keeping with the overall design of the resort. With its natural outdoor features, such as mineral baths and babbling streams, the spa offers a relaxing calm isolated from Seattle, yet just over an hour away. Guests and owners are also able to experience the winter sun and views of the valley from an expansive sun deck on the promontory in front of the lodge.

FOUR SEASONS SCOTTSDALE
AT TROON NORTH

Design/Completion:	2001
Location:	Scottsdale, Arizona
Client:	Four Seasons Hotels & Resorts
Size:	248,000 square feet

Surrounded by the pristine Sonoran desert below the dramatic rock outcroppings of Pinnacle Peak, this Four Seasons resort offers a luxurious Southwestern experience. One of the finest mainland golf destinations, Troon North Golf Club features two 18-hole championship courses designed by Tom Weiskopf.

Blending effortlessly with its majestic desert surroundings, the resort entrance – a traditional adobe hacienda high above Phoenix – welcomes guests with its comfortable Southwestern-inspired lobby living room, fine dining restaurants and meeting facilities.

Each of the 210 guestrooms, including 22 suites situated within 25 one- and two-story adobe casitas, are carefully sited to take advantage of dramatic desert and golf course views, awe-inspiring rock formations and ancient Saguaro cacti forests. Patio doors open to a private landscaped terrace or balcony, each featuring magnificent desert vistas.

The regionally inspired guestroom casita and hotel interiors are influenced by the vibrant palette of the Sonoran desert – colorful, sunset-tinged hues are woven into the fabrics on custom furnishings sourced from Mexican artisans. The resort's public areas showcase handmade art by Huichol Indians and feature traditional hacienda architectural elements including thick plaster walls, arches and viga- and latilla-latticed ceilings of rough-hewn logs.

In addition to golf, this desert oasis offers two pools, tennis, spa, fitness center and 150 acres for outdoor recreation.

THE VENETIAN MACAO-RESORT-HOTEL

Design/Completion: 2007

Location: Macau, China

Client: The Venetian

Size: 10.6 million square feet

Association: RTKL Associates and Wilson & Associates

Thousands of guests, VIPs and members of the media from all over the world have lined up to see and experience the world's largest casino, The Venetian Macao-Resort-Hotel.

The $2.4-billion Venetian Macao gaming resort is a Renaissance-era, Venice-themed resort featuring stunning replicas of Venice landmarks such as St. Mark's Square, the Doge's Palace, Campanile Tower and three indoor canals with gondolas and singing gondoliers.

The entry galleria leads to a grand curved escalator occupying a two-story space at the center of the casino that connects to a shopping center on the upper level. The shopping center is modeled after the Grand Canal Shops at The Venetian in Las Vegas, using themed façades to recreate a Venetian streetscape, complete with canals and gondolas.

The 10.6-million-square-foot Venetian Macao-Resort-Hotel combines the glamour of Las Vegas with mystical Asian flair with 3,000 luxury suites, a 1-million-square-foot convention center, a 15,000-seat arena, a performance theater and many restaurants from fast food to exquisite fine dining. With exclusive VIP suites, a full-service private club, the finest gaming tables in Asia and sophisticated fashion boutiques, this new entertainment destination anchors the new Cotai Strip.

ATLANTIS PHASE II

Design/Completion:	1999
Location:	Paradise Island, Bahamas
Client:	Kerzner International
Size:	1.5 million square feet
Association:	Wimberly Allison Tong & Goo and Wilson & Associates

More than a resort, Atlantis is a destination where architecture and environment have been designed to engage all the senses for interactive entertainment, exploration and discovery. With the world's largest marine habitat, lagoons, waterfalls, a $15-million marina and the largest casino in the Caribbean, the property has achieved a distinct combination of comfort and adventure unlikely to be rivaled.

A complete and multidimensional themed destination resort where every sight, taste and experience seems to immerse the visitor in a mysterious universe, Atlantis was inspired by the myth of the Lost Continent of Atlantis. As if built on the ruins of the legendary city, the 1,208-room Royal Towers rise high above the Paradise Island landscape. Its soaring towers, arches, domes and spires are a fanciful tribute to the legend that inspired them.

Atlantis itself is larger than life, from the 70-foot ceiling of the Great Hall of Waters lobby, to the casino's gaming tables and slot machines swirling around the Temple of the Sun and Temple of the Moon. The exclusive bridge suite, at 5,000 feet above the ground with 360-degree views, may be the most spectacular suite in the world.

One of the hotel's main attractions is the 3.4 million-gallon saltwater habitat including a Predator Lagoon and Reef, 13,000 marine animals representing more than 100 species, 40 waterfalls, two underground grottos for marine life observation and an underwater clear tunnel for close inspection of sharks.

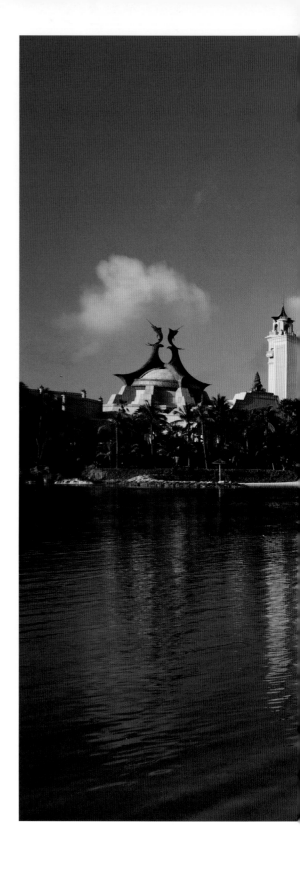

LOEWS VENTANA CANYON RESORT

Design/Completion:	1984
Location:	Tucson, Arizona
Client:	The Estes Company
Size:	n/a

Located on a desert plateau with the scenic Santa Catalina Mountains rising behind the property, the award-winning Loews Ventana Canyon Resort seamlessly embraces the natural surroundings of the breathtaking Sonoran desert. Vertically textured masonry blocks echo the forms of nearby saguaro cacti and the colors of natural rock formations. The resort's 400 rooms and suites step up the hillside's natural contours, allowing guests to experience the rugged natural setting including one of the most dramatic features of the site – an 80-foot waterfall. Guest rooms and suites have balconies with views of distant city lights or mountains. The tranquil and luxurious interiors are accentuated by native flagstone floors and natural fabrics inspired by the richly subdued colors of the Sonoran desert. Resort amenities include a full-service spa, two Tom Fazio golf courses, nature trails and a family-friendly playground.

HILTON ORLANDO CONVENTION CENTER HOTEL

Design/Completion:	2009
Location:	Orlando, Florida
Client:	Hilton Hotels
Size:	1.2 million square feet

Stepping out of the traditional Mediterranean- and Caribbean-themed hotels of Orlando, the Hilton Orlando Convention Center Hotel's design speaks to the local landscape and experience of central Florida, complete with 1,400 guest rooms and over 125,000 square feet of versatile meeting space.

The hotel's unique design creates a rustic atmosphere, contrasting with sleek glass and steel. The roughness of the fieldstone and the meandering, river-like shapes of the pools and walkways provide a fresh and fascinating contrast to the cool, clean lines of the hotel. Generous outdoor terraces and large planes of floor-to-ceiling glass merge outside and inside – creating a one-of-a-kind experience.

Orlando is known for its lakes, ponds and other water features that stretch out into the horizon. Water features play a significant part in the Hilton Orlando experience. The hotel's landscape was designed specifically to make reference to the karst geology, climate and native ecosystem of Florida. Furthering the guest experience is a lazy river with waterfalls, water sprays and mist springs. The pool bar and waterslide structures continue the theme, reflecting the flavor of Florida's native, Cracker style of architecture with lapped siding, metal roofs and fieldstone accents.

JW MARRIOTT SAN ANTONIO

Design/Completion:	2009
Location:	San Antonio, Texas
Client:	JW Marriott
Size:	1.1 million square feet

The JW Marriott San Antonio Resort celebrates and reflects the rich cultural history and natural beauty of the Texas Hill Country, resulting in a setting that is comfortable and contemporary, yet true to its Texas roots.

The hotel offers 1,002 spacious rooms; a three-level, 370,000-square-foot conference facility with an expo hall, ballrooms and 125,000 square feet of elegant meeting space; a luxurious spa area; upscale fitness facilities; and retail areas. A three-meal restaurant, sports bar and grill and a specialty steakhouse restaurant cater to a wide variety of culinary tastes.

The hotel is built from indigenous stone as well as local woods including pecan, mesquite and oak. Inside, the palette of carpets, furniture, drapes and other accessories draws inspiration from the wildflowers that cover the surrounding hills during the spring and early summer. Richly textured woods, rock and hand-crafted metal embody simple elegance and enduring strength.

The materials and building techniques reflect the traditional European craftsmanship of the area's German settlers. The traditional Spanish hacienda style is a more subtle presence, reflected in the large verandas, comfortable public areas, peaceful courtyards and intimate gardens. Created historic structures complete the bond between the past and a contemporary sense of comfort.

HYATT LOST PINES RESORT AND SPA

Design/Completion:	2006
Location:	Lost Pines, Texas
Client:	Hyatt Hotels & Resorts
Size:	480,000 square feet

Located at a bend in the Colorado River, Hyatt Regency Lost Pines Resort and Spa balances the agrarian history of the local Texas ranches with the delicate natural features that exist throughout the site. Guests arrive at the 491-guest-room resort through a forest of native pine trees. Incorporating elements of local historic architecture, the resort offers countless amenities to allow guests to fully experience the Texas spirit.

The resort includes 57 suites, a presidential house, 60,000 square feet of meeting space, two ballrooms, a fine dining restaurant and five other restaurants and bars. The presidential suite, set apart from the main building, offers open-air corridors and deep porches for a truly authentic experience.

The main building is a series of low-scale guestroom wings designed to look like separate buildings built over time. Local vernacular including wood-sided, wrap-around porches with sky-blue painted ceilings, shingled roofs and traditional stone fixtures allow the resort to tell the story of Texas. Multi-paned, floor-to-ceiling windows allow guests to discover nature's splendor from every angle. The full-service spa, designed with a more contemporary feel through the use of lines and varied roof forms, offers relaxation through serene views of the lake and an outdoor courtyard. Additional hotel amenities include a golf course, water park, horseback riding center and an open-air pavilion.

4 | PLAY

Cowboys Stadium	204
Lucas Oil Stadium	210
Pizza Hut Park	216
Garland Special Events Center	218
Jersey Boys Theatre	222
Dodger Stadium	226
D.C. United Soccer Stadium	228
Amon G. Carter Stadium Master Plan	230
Liverpool FC Stadium	232
Territorio Santos Modelo – Estadio Corona	236
Proposed 2014 World Cup Venue	238
Estádio do Maracanã	242
Camelback Ranch	246

COWBOYS STADIUM

Design/Completion: 2009

Location: Arlington, Texas

Client: Dallas Cowboys Football Club

Size: 3 million square feet

The new Cowboys Stadium stands as a monumental physical expression of the team: dominant and powerful in stature, simple and purposeful in nature. Its architecture dwells in modernism – purity of form, structural expression, functional clarity and true innovation.

Swift form, powerful structure and agile movement serve as strong links between the architectural form of the building and the primary use of the venue. The stadium is the largest NFL venue ever built, boasting the most spectacular column-free room in the world – stretching a quarter-mile in length. The retractable roof is designed to emulate Texas Stadium's famous hole in the roof, and the end zones feature the largest retractable doors in the world, measuring 120 feet high by 180 feet wide.

The center-hung video board spans between the 20 yard lines and features four individual boards, facing the sidelines and end zones. The stadium includes 350 private luxury suites, The Dallas Cowboys Hall of Fame and a Dallas Cowboys Pro Shop. From the longest single-span roof structure in the world to the canted glass wall that creates an ever-changing aesthetic depending on the time of day, no architectural expression is more appropriate for the Dallas Cowboys.

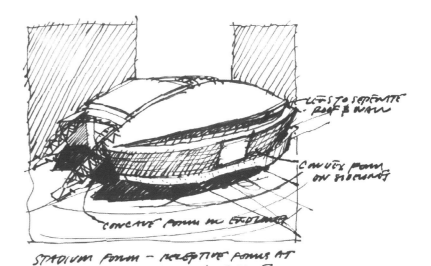

STADIUM FORM — RECEPTIVE FORMS AT
ENDZONE — CONVEX ON SIDELINES

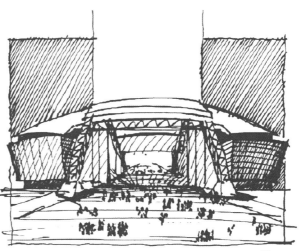

NORTH ENDZONE — ALL ON DIFFERENT FLOORS
ANY FACILITY — MECHANICAL AND PEDESTRIAN FLOW.

LUCAS OIL STADIUM

Design/Completion: 2008

Location: Indianapolis, Indiana

Client: Indiana Stadium & Convention Building Authority

Size: 1.9 million square feet

Taking architectural energy from the city and state's rich heritage, Lucas Oil Stadium imparts a civility to conjure a turn-of-the-century field house/stadium aesthetic for one for the most distinctive multi-use mega-venues in the world.

This landmark combines a palette of simple forms and materials indigenous to the region to create a fitting contextual expression for the city of Indianapolis. The design portrays purity of form, structural expression, functional clarity and the integration of cutting-edge technological materials, methods and equipment. The design for the stadium's exterior harkens back to Indiana's rich sports heritage while enhancing its urban, downtown Indianapolis location.

The 63,000-seat multi-use stadium, home of the NFL's Indianapolis Colts, offers convention and assembly space and includes the first center court design for the NCAA Final Four tournament. Looking out over Monument Circle, the glass doors, the first in the NFL, measure 110 feet high by 88 feet wide. Lucas Oil Stadium incorporates aspects from some of today's great stadiums while creating a design that offers timeless elegance and warmth.

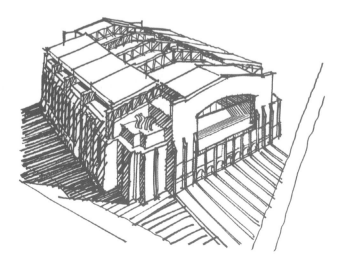

PIZZA HUT PARK

Design/Completion:	2005
Location:	Frisco, Texas
Client:	Hunt Sports Group, FC Dallas, the City of Frisco,
	Frisco Independent School District, and Collin County
Size:	1.5 million square feet

Pizza Hut Park, a unique 117-acre facility, is the first of its kind in the U.S. The park features a 21,193-person soccer-specific stadium that hosts all home FC Dallas MLS matches, U.S. Men's and Women's National Team, international matches, major concert events, Frisco High School football games and additional community events. Adjacent to the stadium are 17 championship-quality soccer fields that are available year-round to host amateur teams and serve as the playing site of regional, national and international soccer competitions.

FC Dallas and Hunt Sports Group developed a unique partnership with the Frisco Independent School District, the City of Frisco and Collin County to build the stadium and adjacent soccer complex.

The stadium is composed of materials and forms familiar to Texas' unique architectural style. Stone, steel and concrete are combined to create shaded areas at the stadium's entries and concourses. The large 'Texas porch,' which signifies the entry to the west stand, recalls the deep shaded porches that mark so many of Texas' most important civil structures. The stadium's interior concourses are designed to make fans feel they are in the game by providing uninterrupted, 360-degree views from any point around the field.

GARLAND SPECIAL EVENTS CENTER

Design/Completion: 2005

Location: Garland, Texas

Client: Garland Independent School District

Size: 190,000 square feet

The Garland Special Events Center is designed to meet the school district's need for a modern multi-use facility to accommodate graduations, sporting events and district-wide conferences. The contemporary design reflects the progressive thinking of the school district and the surrounding community.

The building form resolves the problem of programmatic function and the desire to create a cohesive whole by the varied use of opacity and transparency. Those spaces requiring blackout conditions – ballroom, lecture hall and field house – are housed behind opaque masonry and mill-finished aluminum blocks, while the grand entry and main concourse space are wrapped in large expanses of sweeping canted glazing.

The main roof's gently arcing form serves two purposes. By juxtaposing it against the sweeping glass, the sense of movement is enhanced, and at the same time acts as a unifying element to tie programmatic functions into a single form. The large projecting canopies act to reinforce and extend the building's horizontal expression.

The building's dynamic form is further enhanced on the interior by expressing and celebrating its structural skeleton by the use of tree-like columns and by the use of colored LED lighting on the interior and exterior.

JERSEY BOYS THEATRE

Design/Completion: 2008

Location: Las Vegas, Nevada

Client: Las Vegas Sands Corp.

Size: 70,000 square feet

Enter this energized, sculptural environment and be transported to another place in time. Where are you? At the new Las Vegas venue designed for the Tony Award-winning musical Jersey Boys. The 1,700-seat theater was custom designed and built as the premier performance showroom for the new Palazzo Resort Hotel Casino.

The conceptual design was developed to tip a whimsical nod in tribute to the world-renowned musical group for which it was designed. The entry portal was inspired by a 1960s automobile taillight with concession stands that hearken back to the same time.

Layers of sculpted forms and liquid planes blend with bold, iconic graphic textures. Form and space transition harmoniously like the decades of music highlighted in the show. The uniquely choreographed infusion of details and materials recall theaters of yesterday spun to create a hip, club-style atmosphere drawing today's crowd to one of the hottest shows on the Las Vegas Strip.

The space also includes many sustainable elements such as a sparkling recycled glass and mirror terrazzo floor, tiled walls with glass fabricated from recycled car windshields, coil draperies recycled from a former Venetian museum space and light-reflecting sustainable resin wall panels.

PLAY | JERSEY BOYS THEATRE 223

DODGER STADIUM

Design/Completion: 2012

Location: Los Angeles, California

Client: Los Angeles Dodgers

Size: n/a

Dodger Stadium, one of baseball and Southern California's most esteemed venues, is being updated nearly 50 years after its original opening. The renovation has strengthened and enhanced not only the history of the venue, but also the mid-century modern architectural style of the stadium's original form.

At the same time, improvements have provided fans with all of the amenities that one would expect to find at a state-of-the-art facility. The first phase of the renovation brought back the stadium's most distinctive feature, its original four pastel color seating. This phase of renovation also saw the creation of baseline box seating, which used mid-century modern forms and materials to create a period-appropriate renovation that complements the southern Californian's outdoor lifestyle.

Providing a mid-century vision where none had existed, the renovation of the field level concourse was undertaken to create a clean, streamlined concourse achieving a complementary balance between the bowl and the strong exterior style of the stadium. Frank McCourt, owner of the Dodgers, put it best when he stated, "We're creating a new stadium without tearing down the old with a renovation that honors the history by protecting and modernizing Dodger Stadium for years to come."

D.C. UNITED SOCCER STADIUM

Design/Completion:	n/a
Location:	Washington, D.C.
Client:	D.C. United Soccer
Size:	755,000 square feet

Designed as part of an urban master plan, the D.C. United soccer stadium is part of a mixed-use development near the nation's Capitol. The proposed soccer stadium is enveloped on three sides by commercial buildings that define much of the facility's exterior. The interrelationship between the stadium and these other facilities is most evident with the conference hotel along the west façade.

The main entrance to the stadium opens to a dynamic, six-story atrium with views to the club, suites and hotel rooms above. The hotel lobby serves as the entrance for suite and club seat members and the hotel restaurant doubles as the club on game days. Additionally, conference rooms can be used as hospitality rooms for pre-game and post-game activities.

Designed in the tradition of European soccer venues, particularly in the seating bowl configuration, the rake of the seats on the east side of the field is steeper, creating an intimidating environment for visiting teams. The seats at the north end retract to create a stage for concerts, covered by a large, flowing roof canopy, symbolic of the eagle on the team crest. The glass façade on the stadium's east side houses the team's administrative offices and looks out over the practice facility.

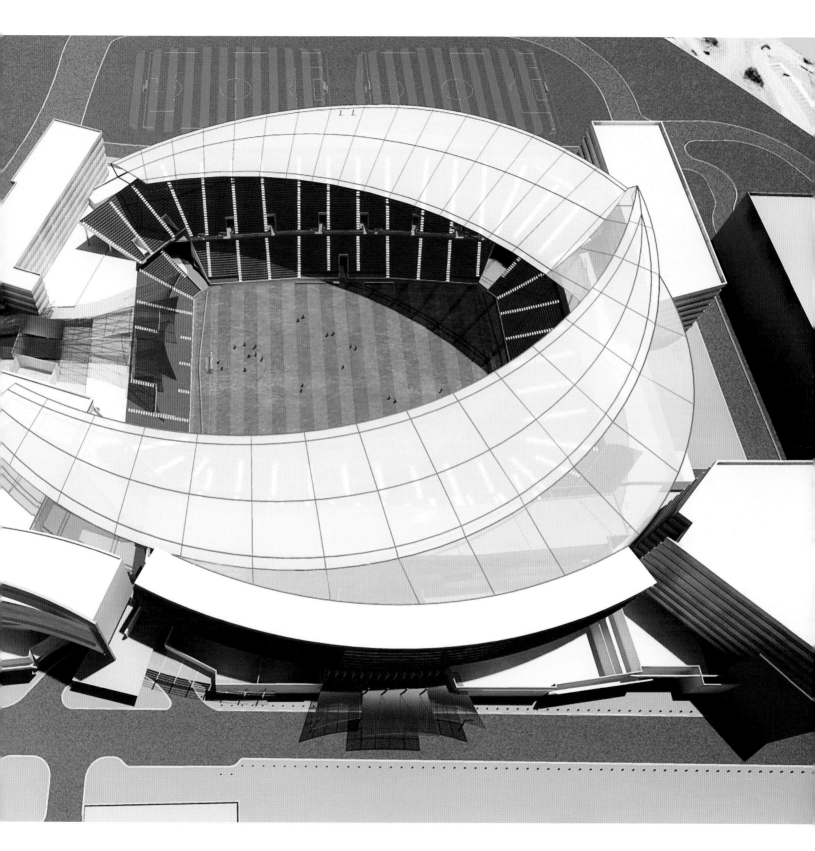

AMON G. CARTER STADIUM MASTER PLAN

Design/Completion: 2009

Location: Fort Worth, Texas

Client: Texas Christian University

Size: 500,000 square feet

As the dominant physical symbol of the Texas Christian University (TCU) football program, Amon G. Carter Stadium stands as a visible landmark throughout the Fort Worth area.

Developed from research of the original 1920s architectural design, the stadium's master plan reflects the southwestern art deco style found extensively throughout the TCU campus as well as the Fort Worth central business district.

The plan preserves the intimacy and scale of Amon G. Carter Stadium while integrating it with the adjacent Daniel Meyer Coliseum, Justin Athletic Center, Walsh Performance Complex and the Sam Baugh Indoor Practice Facility. This creates a unique on-campus sports complex for football and basketball.

The stadium, which will be renovated in phases, is designed around the concept of a 360-degree view of the field from the main concourse. This approach keeps the fans in touch with the action at all times. Also incorporated into the renovations will be luxury suites, loge boxes and club seating, club lounges, party decks, new and enlarged press facilities and concourse amenities.

LIVERPOOL FC STADIUM

Design/Completion:	n/a
Location:	Liverpool, England
Client:	Liverpool Football Club
Size:	1.6 million square feet

Liverpool Football Club is one of the most successful clubs in Europe. Its acquisition by American owners coincided with Liverpool's period as the European City of Culture. The new ownership decided that substantial expansion was necessary and a new state-of-the-art stadium was required.

In response, HKS provided a design unique to this club. The building is intended to become an icon among football stadiums worldwide – encapsulating the culture and character of the club, its city and the tradition of English football. As such, the design makes sense at this site and only this site.

Major design generators include the Kop (a single-tier, 20,000-seat stand behind home goal) from which the entire asymmetrical plan hangs, and which provides the internal focus for the bowl. Externally, the corners are cut away to provide clearly identifiable stands to each side of the pitch, allow the park to penetrate the building, provide public views into the stadium and increase the sense of this as a public facility.

The stadium contains community facilities, accommodation for the sports faculty of John Moore's University, a museum shop and a cafeteria. The south end (the back of the Kop) forms a civic presence onto what will become a public plaza following the demolition of the existing stadium.

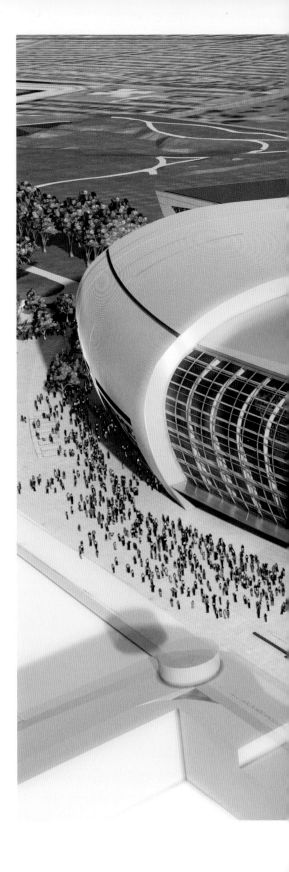

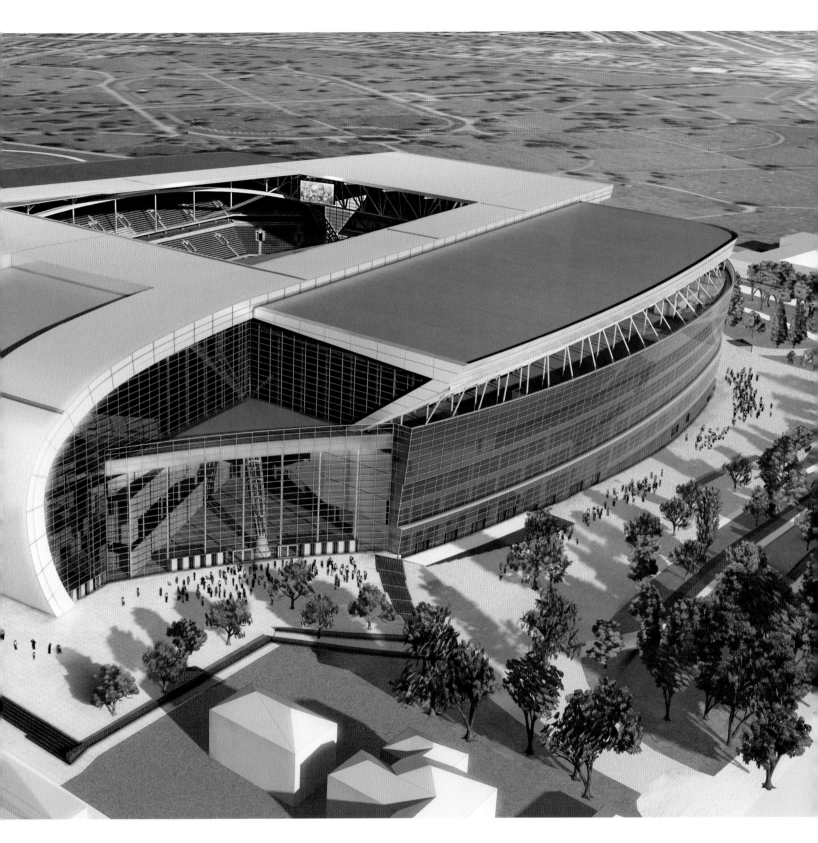

TERRITORIO SANTOS
MODELO–ESTADIO CORONA

Design/Completion:	2009
Location:	Torreón Coahulia, Mexico
Client:	Grupo Modelo
Size:	2.2 million square feet

Estadio Corona's design will create a vibrant new home for Santos Laguna, one of the premier soccer teams in Mexico. Inspired by the city of Torreón's industrial character and desert terrain, the stadium consists of a series of gentle curves that embrace and shelter the sacred playing field.

The long, serpentine steel wall on the eastern side cuts the ground as it moves along the field and appears as a ring of fire as the sun sets in the west. The west façade functions as the main gateway to the stadium, and the use of stone at the base anchors the building while the tubular zinc mesh creates a soft screen that shines and hovers with the sun.

The use of local and regional materials throughout the exterior of the stadium unifies the sense of place and secures the stadium as a symbol of renewal in the region. The game experience is enhanced by creating a continuous, elongated bowl and bringing the seats as close to the action as possible while the fabric roof becomes softly lit at night to symbolize the saints' auras over the sacred field.

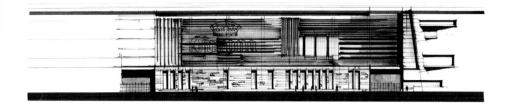

PROPOSED 2014 WORLD CUP VENUE

Design/Completion: 2013
Location: Brazil
Client: Confidential
Size: 600,000 square feet

The proposed venue for the 2014 FIFA World Cup is designed to acknowledge the context of place, contemporary Brazilian landscape design and the heroic modernism of the recent past.

A sweeping greenbelt park intersects with the stadium site, integrating the stadium with the landscape, while surrounding park spaces rise to an uplifted promenade level. The open promenade, elevated on a berm, creates a podium for the stadium's spatial hierarchies and sculptural shapes that rise and float above the podium and the ascending sculpted landforms.

The forms and spatial organization acknowledge the influence and spirit of Brazil's heroic modernism. Large-scale asymmetrical struts cross the garden rooms, further defining the exterior spaces and supporting the cantilevered exterior wall with a dynamic tension.

The stadium will feature a full range of premium seating areas including suites, club seats and mini-suites. The premium areas will be supported by amenities including club spaces, pubs and restaurants. The promenade and open ends offer opportunities to create event-specific concession villages or temporary seating areas to expand the stadium's seating capacity for larger events. The venue is designed to be flexible and is capable of hosting sporting events and musical performances.

ESTÁDIO DO MARACANÃ

Design/Completion: 2013
Location: Rio de Janeiro, RJ, Brazil
Client: Odebrecht and International Stadia Group
Size: 1 million square feet

Set within the heart of Rio de Janeiro, Maracanã Stadium's monumental ramps, iconic cantilevered roof and bowl shape are dramatic interventions in the urban fabric. Design concepts for renovations are guided by the urban setting and a desire to preserve an iconic, historic stadium with a rich, vibrant cultural heritage.

Built for the 1950 FIFA World Cup, the Maracanã has been the setting for many of Brazilian football's greatest moments. A new roof will be suspended above the stadium providing weather protection for the majority of the seats, and becoming a metaphorical cloud creating a canvas of light for new media technologies.

A reorganization of the stadium circulation will return the ascending monumental ramps to the fan base while the exit ramp towers will have a dynamic media façade creating a dramatic media environment. The new premium seating areas will include suites, loge boxes, club seats, restaurants and hospitality areas along with a museum celebrating the history of Brazilian football.

Sculptural pebble-shaped garages providing safe, secure parking mimic the surrounding mountains and the existing stadium plan. Monumental urban plazas and terraces designed as gathering spaces will offer retail, theaters, food kiosks and areas for special events. Once complete, Brazilian football fans will once again enjoy the dramatic views of Rio de Janeiro from the top of "The Temple of the Brazilian Football Gods."

CAMELBACK RANCH

Design/Completion: 2009

Location: Phoenix, Arizona

Client: Arizona Diamondbacks, Los Angeles Dodgers

Size: 234,000 square feet

The $100 million Camelback Ranch Spring Training Facility for the Chicago White Sox and the Los Angeles Dodgers is designed with 10,000 fixed seats and 3,000 lawn seats, making it the largest facility in the state's Cactus League.

The innovative campus setting is designed with contemporary southwestern desert architecture, offering the best in training facilities for two of Major League Baseball's most storied teams as well as a destination location for the entire community.

The site, which is organized around a central connecting path and lake, hosts two stadium entries – one at home plate and a more prominent entry at center field. The stadium concourse is open with views into the stadium as well as broad walkways. Both the stadium and the entire site are designed as pedestrian experiences.

Located on a 141-acre site with a 3-acre lake, the stadium has the capacity to host 13,000 fans. It includes more than 118,000 square feet of clubhouses as well as four major league practice fields, eight minor league practice fields and two practice infields. Each team has a replica major league field to emulate their home stadium.

5 | WORK

Abu Dhabi Financial Centre – Luxury Hotel & Residences   252

Post Oak Mixed-Use Development   256

Corporate Office Building   258

Hall Arts Center   264

Civica Plaza   266

Veleiro do Sul Skyscraper   268

Northpark Center   270

Terrace V   274

ABU DHABI FINANCIAL CENTRE – LUXURY HOTEL & RESIDENCES

Design/Completion: 2007
Location: Abu Dhabi, United Arab Emirates
Client: Abu Dhabi Financial Centre
Size: 95,000 square feet

The guest experience of the Abu Dhabi Financial Centre – Luxury Hotel & Residences begins from afar as the tower stands tall as a landmark to the financial district and continues with the elevated arrival court raised above the main street, which alleviates the visual and audible distractions created by the high-volume traffic from the street.

Rising above a refined and simple rectangular hotel building mass, the residential tower extrudes itself as two split-radial masses symmetrically organized on a central axis, offering a softer edge against the Abu Dhabi sky. The southern-most radial tower extends from the symmetry, rising above the residential floors and providing a clear separation and identity for the more exclusive owners. A private penthouse rooftop pool and heliport top the tower.

The amenity deck with infinity-edge pool – one of the project's signature design elements – boldly extends from the base of the tower and overlooks the water-front and marina below. Views from the project capture the Arabian Sea, rolling sculpture gardens and an uninterrupted skyline of downtown Abu Dhabi.

The Abu Dhabi Financial Centre – Luxury Hotel & Residences is intended to be a world-renowned architectural icon for Abu Dhabi, a gateway to Al Suwwah Island and a landmark to the Abu Dhabi Financial District.

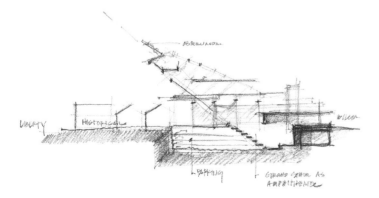

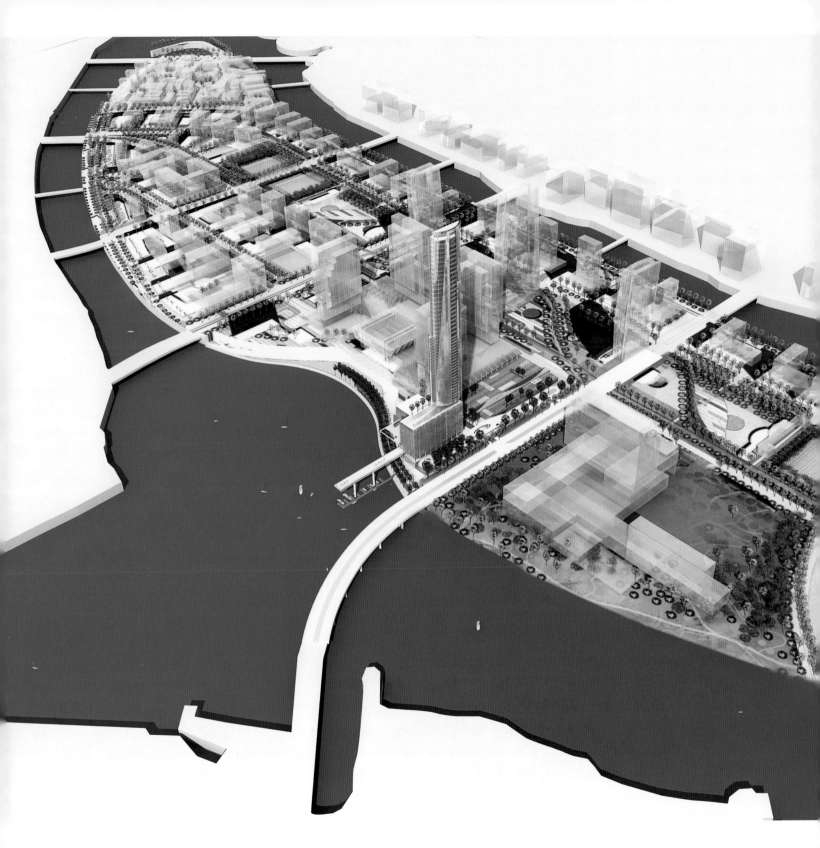

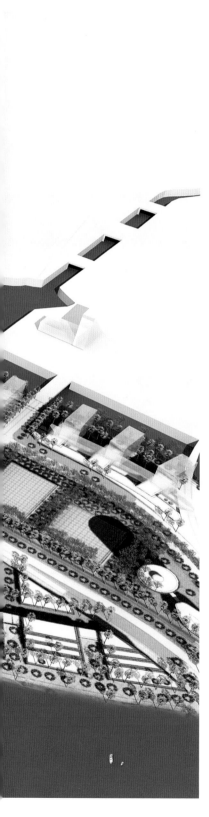

WORK | ABU DHABI FINANCIAL CENTRE – LUXURY HOTEL & RESIDENCES   255

POST OAK MIXED-USE DEVELOPMENT

Design/Completion: 2008
Location: Houston, Texas
Client: Redstone Companies, Stream Realty
Size: 1.6 million square feet

The design solution for Post Oak Mixed-Use Development achieves a holistic synchronization of all realms. A new all-inclusive urban community stands to re-ignite Houston's flourishing uptown neighborhood.

A park, surrounded by three elegant towers, becomes the development's Central Park – providing an escape for guests, office users and residents alike. The architecture provides a pure and timeless aesthetic against the open skies of Houston. High-end retail shops lining the park bring a Rodeo Drive flair to Houston's famous Galleria area.

The hotel is the cornerstone of the development, bringing in a high level of sophistication and service. The rooftop energizes the project with an activated outdoor space. An aquarium pool with clear glass walls allows guests to over-look Houston's blanket of treetops even while swimming underwater.

CORPORATE OFFICE BUILDING

Design/Completion:	2006
Location:	Southfield, Michigan
Client:	Confidential
Size:	110,000 square feet
Association:	Albert Kahn Associates

With considerable concern about manufacturing jobs and companies relocating from Michigan to other states and countries, this company decided to remain in Southfield. The firm expanded and built a new headquarters on a 36-acre site – adjacent to its existing 25-acre campus.

The park-like environment links the new 110,000-square-foot headquarters building to existing business units, allowing the firm to consolidate purchasing, engineering and design studios while publicly enhancing its brand. The master plan provides for additional facilities in the future while maintaining the park-like setting. The organizing site wall is a terracotta rain-screen and the primary building materials are coated aluminum and low-E glass.

Facing the street and hovering over the site wall is a textured glass panel screen. The façades oriented toward the garden are fully glass – utilizing a low-iron glazing and providing clarity to the private view. The lobby features a three-story, glass-enclosed communicating stair adjacent to a 300-seat auditorium and dining facility, which extends outside to the garden. The executive floor also maintains a strong orientation to the garden with both a balcony and a tall skylit space at the periphery of each office. Automobiles featuring the company's product line are exhibited in the lobby.

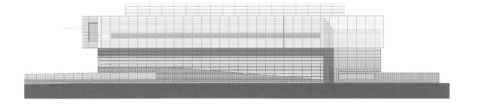

HALL ARTS CENTER

Design/Completion:	2008
Location:	Dallas, Texas
Client:	Hall Financial Group
Size:	1 million square feet

Positioned at the heart of the world-renowned Dallas Arts District, Hall Arts Center finds itself surrounded by iconic landmark buildings designed by four critically acclaimed Pritzker Prize-winning architects (Piano, Pei, Foster and Koolhaas). In an effort for this project to live up to the quality and high expectations of its neighbors, the design aims for a timeless international aesthetic.

Hall Arts Center marks the skyline with two towers comprised of office and residential rising above a simple yet elegantly detailed glass podium that contributes to the district's synergy through restaurants, public space and a sculpture garden. Due to the distinct site location and the connection with the arts, the design was inspired by the idea of art and the vision of incorporating elements of art as an integral expression of the design.

To create an iconic presence against the Dallas skyline, the art concept is revealed with a five-story glass box that appears to slice through the office tower's double-skin façade. The towers incorporate a double-skin curtainwall system as a sustainable concept that shields the towers from direct solar heat gain. The design of the double skin symbolizes an international style of architecture celebrating the quality, sophistication and elegance of the Dallas Arts District.

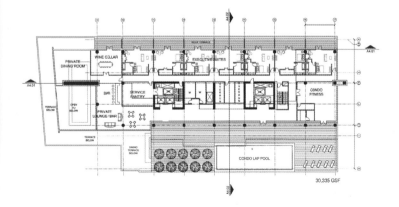

CIVICA PLAZA

Design/Completion: 2006

Location: Coral Gables, Florida

Client: Swerdlow Group

Size: 1.2 million square feet

Located within the medical research district of the University of Miami, Civica Plaza is a unique mixed-use development that incorporates office and medical office space, retail and covered parking.

A row of palms extends the flavor of the Coral Gables community through the site and visually buffers the building from traffic. An arcade at street level creates a protected but transparent promenade lined with shops and cafés with outdoor seating. The ground plane is an energetic environment that provides opportunities for chance meetings and casual conversation.

Due to the irregular shape of the site, the parking garage translates the trapezoid-shaped footprint vertically until it reaches the tower. The tower rationalizes the floor plates into a series of orthogonal profiles. Glass corners protrude outward to express the larger suites.

Layered skins, notches and slits along the envelope create a variety of outdoor balcony conditions that frame views of the Miami skyline and maximize corner office opportunities. Fins, part of the exoskeleton condition of the building, articulate the façade by adding a finer degree of detail and creating intricate shadows that contrast the reflective nature of the metal and glass when exposed to the sun.

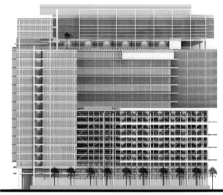

south

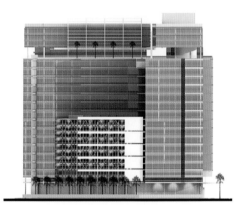

west

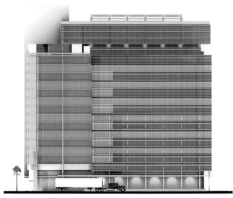

east

VELEIRO DO SUL SKYSCRAPER

Design/Completion:	2006
Location:	Rio de Janeiro, RJ, Brazil
Client:	eVolo International Design Competition
Size:	1.3 million square feet

Three factors were used as main design parameters: symbolism, culture and context. The symbolism began from the term skyscraper, which was originally a nautical term used well before high rises came about, to refer to the tallest mast on a ship.

Culture is important because Brazilians are known for enjoying the outdoors, sun and nature and for having a fascinating reluctance for interior spaces. The context provided gentle breezes, spectacular sunsets and amazing vistas of the Bay of Guanabara, the Sugar Loaf Mountain, the Christ atop Corcovado Mountain, Flamengo beach and embankment as well as the beautiful Marina da Glória.

The tower's main feature is a sail-like device, comprised of turbines spun by the wind, thus generating the energy used in the building. This concept is a poetic and symbolic response to the sails of ships, and it helps blend the nautical-looking design with the bay and the marina. Oversized terraces were carefully balanced with large glass expanses that were spread throughout the building to provide family-gathering areas, thus enabling the building to open up to the exterior, engaging its context and the local culture as well as challenging the established idea of an enclosed space.

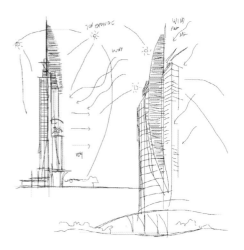

NORTHPARK CENTER

Design/Completion: 2008
Location: Dallas, Texas
Client: NorthPark Center
Size: 2.4 million square feet

Sited adjacent to the existing NorthPark Mall, the NorthPark Center expansion seeks to address both functional programmatic needs as well as a timeless sophisticated aesthetic. Providing a 300-key boutique hotel with 25,000 square feet of conference space, 2 million square feet of office lease space, 300,000 square feet of additional retail, 9,200 parking spaces and a 10-acre structured deck park, the project also improves, in addition to NorthPark's physical size, the quality of the user experience. Through careful examination of current patron experience, including vehicular arrival, parking, entry and circulation patterns, a holistic solution was derived that enhances all aspects of this experience.

With a linear axis stretching from the east to west edges of the site, the deck park cradles energy between the two office tower components that bookmark each end, maximizing the park opportunity. Flanked to the north by a boutique hotel and amenities, the park offers relaxing respite from street life for both hotel guests and retail patrons. Retail defines the edges of the park and offers a variety of specialty shopping destinations and restaurants, which line the front of the park and utilize the adjacent outdoor area for seating and dining. Offering multiple zones of varying size and proportion, the park itself becomes an extension of the capabilities of the existing courtyard space within the mall – a place to display and experience fashion and sculpture and stage outdoor events.

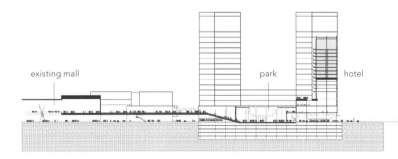

existing mall   park   hotel

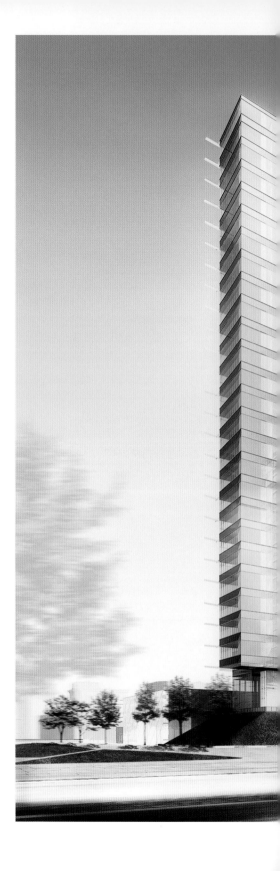

TERRACE V

Design/Completion: 2009
Location: Austin, Texas
Client: The Terrace
Size: 220,000 square feet

Terrace V sits high on a bluff above Barton Creek in southwest Austin, Texas, overlooking the Texas Hill Country to the west and downtown Austin to the northeast. The Terrace, a 100-acre, 1.1-million-square-foot master-planned office complex, currently consists of four office buildings and will ultimately grow to seven buildings in all. Terrace V is designed to flow naturally from its Hill Country environment and to feel as though it belongs within the existing campus. However, at the same time, it creates its own new and unique identity.

Seeking a minimum LEED-Silver certification from the U.S. Green Building Council and a 3-Star rating through the Austin Energy Green Building program, the design is strongly influenced by an effort to achieve this sustainability by using elements such as local materials and finishes, horizontal and vertical shading devices and extensive use of native landscaping.

A speculative office building, Terrace V, with seven stories of office space, has a highly flexible and efficient 31,500-square-foot floor plate. With optimal bay spacing and core layout, it has the ability to perform for a wide variety of prospective tenants. Its top floor, recessed back to expose large shaded balconies, takes advantage of the outstanding views. Its soft, flowing lines are created by large, curving sheets of glass dynamically layered over vertically articulated precast concrete masses with intersecting native limestone walls that connect the building to the predominant rock outcroppings of the site.

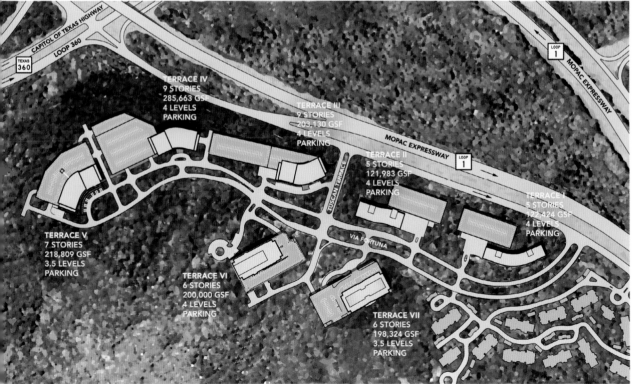

TERRACE IV
9 STORIES
285,663 GSF
4 LEVELS
PARKING

TERRACE III
9 STORIES
203,130 GSF
4 LEVELS
PARKING

TERRACE II
5 STORIES
121,983 GSF
4 LEVELS
PARKING

TERRACE I
5 STORIES
122,424 GSF
4 LEVELS
PARKING

TERRACE V
7 STORIES
218,809 GSF
3.5 LEVELS
PARKING

TERRACE VI
6 STORIES
200,000 GSF
4 LEVELS
PARKING

TERRACE VII
6 STORIES
198,324 GSF
3.5 LEVELS
PARKING

CAPITOL OF TEXAS HIGHWAY

LOOP 360

TEXAS 360

MOPAC EXPRESSWAY

LOOP 1

TUSCAN TERRACE

VIA FORTUNA

6 | LEARN

Center for BrainHealth	280
Kent Building Schools for the Future	284
University of Central Florida Physical Sciences Building	288
Museo del Niño – Parque Ecológico Chapultepec	290
Eastfield College Learning Center	294
Comprehensive Cancer Center	298
Erbil Iraq Schools	302
Academic Teaching Hospital	304
Charles E. Schmidt Medical Center – Master Plan	308
The College of North West London, Wembley Campus	314
UK Medical Centre for Research and Innovation	318
The Center for American and International Law	324

CENTER FOR BRAINHEALTH

Design/Completion:	2008
Location:	Dallas, Texas
Client:	University of Texas, Center for BrainHealth
Size:	63,000 square feet

When renovating a circa-1970 building, architects worked with the client to create a special place for one of the nation's most innovative brain research programs. The design approach creates synergy between the scientific research, the building's image and its connection to the site.

To create a physical identity that symbolically mirrors the mysteries of brain research while exposing the geometric form of the building, the original concrete skin was replaced by perforated copper sunscreens and reflective glass.

The copper sunscreens create a distinct image while protecting the building from direct sunlight. Exposing the cylindrical steel columns was a nod to the original architecture. The burgundy columns are inspired by the original color of the steel beneath.

Two lobby entries allow easy access and provide open views to the landscape. The interior space was integrally designed with the landscape to reinforce connection to the site. The entry lobby provides a dynamic first impression with its open structure painted black and defined by white floating planes, dramatic natural lighting and sophisticated artwork. Pavers were placed atop the existing parking surface to save trees that exist on-site. An outdoor garden functions as an assembly space. The building houses more than 200 researchers.

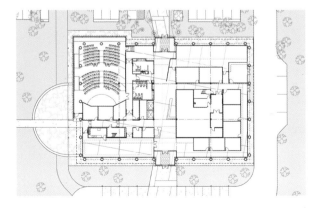

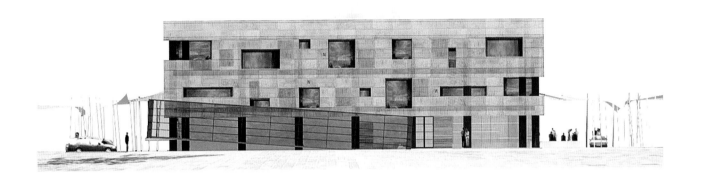

KENT BUILDING SCHOOLS
FOR THE FUTURE

Design/Completion:	2010
Location:	Kent, England
Client:	Kent County Council
Size:	439,000 square feet

Kent County Council (KCC), as part of Wave 3 government Building Schools for the Future (BSF), has secured £750 million for redevelopment of 35 secondary schools in the Thanet and Gravesham area in North Kent. KCC views this as a vital opportunity to regenerate declining communities with new learning and community facilities. Through BSF, KCC's goal is to nurture autonomous and creative learners. HKS Architects is part of the Land Securities Trillium consortium, including construction partner Kier. Two projects are new-build PFI schools and two are D&B refurbishment. Designs for a new all-through school as part of the ongoing partnership are also underway. HKS has created design solutions in conjunction with schools' stakeholders. In working with these groups, HKS has drawn on the work of Fielding and Nair, who in *The Language of School Design*, created a new typology for learning space and naming those spaces. The design team used this tool to prompt debate among participating stakeholders. With the increasing opportunities offered, the team felt it was crucial to use new methods and language to discuss options for the internal design of new facilities to avoid simply delivering a new version of an old solution.

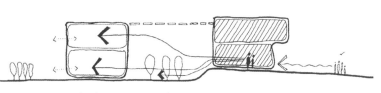

homebases   green heart   the launch pad

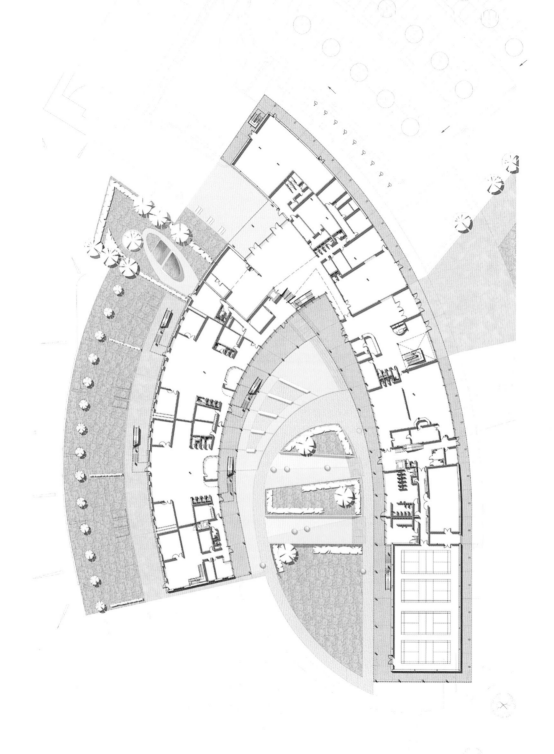

UNIVERSITY OF CENTRAL FLORIDA PHYSICAL SCIENCES BUILDING

Design/Completion:	2007
Location:	Orlando, Florida
Client:	University of Central Florida
Size:	72,000 square feet

The Physical Sciences Building at the University of Central Florida offers students the best and most advanced working environments. The four-story building will house labs for both chemistry and physics research as well as provide new office space for faculty.

The building fosters collaborative working environments by way of its planning while harmoniously coexisting with the environment by way of its architecture. The plan consists of two embracing L shapes. One piece contains teaching labs with support while the other holds offices and research labs.

The result of the interlocking shapes creates a void at the center. This void or outdoor room is a flexible space meant for teaching, gathering, lounging, sleeping, eating and celebrating. It also functions as a light well so that every occupied room can contain at least one window.

Breezeways draw cool air into the courtyard and vent the warmer air out the top. A pedestrian corridor runs along the south end of the site. Visual connectivity to the interior from the south was highly desired but the heat gain was not.

Approaching the entry, the L shape is reintroduced and referenced in the vertical plane. This element shades the four-story lobby space located behind the glass curtainwall and frames the primary entry point.

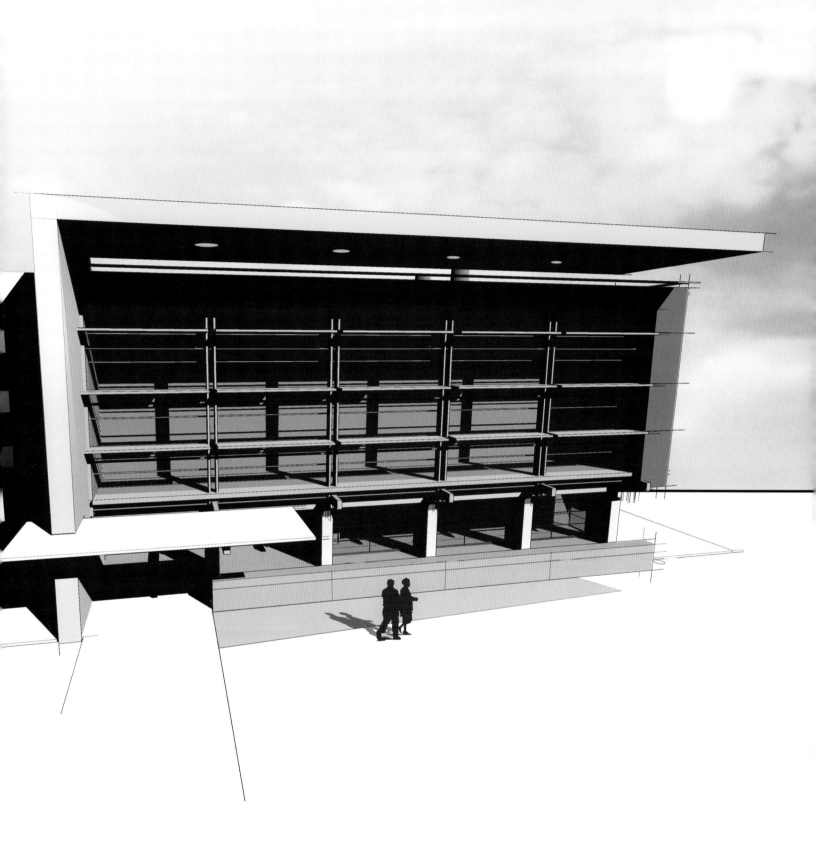

MUSEO DEL NIÑO–PARQUE ECOLÓGICO CHAPULTEPEC

Design/Completion:	2010
Location:	Cuernavaca, Morelos, Mexico
Client:	Museo Interactivo Infantil A.C.
Size:	40,000 square feet

The Museo del Niño – Parque Ecológico Chapultepec, located within the ecological park of Chapultepec, Morelos, is the one of the new centennial and bicentennial projects dedicated to the celebrations of the Mexican Independence and Revolution, respectively. The project design will try to accomplish LEED-Gold certification or above as a result of its commitment to the park.

In a world where children and families struggle to find places to reconnect with nature, this park becomes a natural sanctuary for the city's families. It is one of the most beautiful natural ecosystems in the Valley of Cuernavaca. The project includes the removal of the majority of existing buildings, keeping the ones with most potential.

The existing convention center will become the project's main attraction. Curved glass and steel, in a freeform shape, will become the envelope of the main hall and retail spaces. Four pavilions, which include water, wind, sun and life, become beacons of an architectural gesture of tremendous respect to its environment, lifting themselves from the ground and becoming entities that house the different exhibits. The museum is intended to become one of the leading ecological children's museums in Mexico, and an example for other museums around the world.

EASTFIELD COLLEGE LEARNING CENTER

Design/Completion: 2008

Location: Mesquite, Texas

Client: Dallas County Community College District

Size: 55,000 square feet

The Eastfield College Learning Center is designed to reflect the concept that learning can occur anywhere on campus. The progressive classroom and administrative office facility represents a new initiative to promote knowledge gained through interactive learning environments beyond the traditional classroom.

Studio spaces vary in size, are technology-intense and have an informal feel. The pathway circulation system connecting these spaces is activated with a variety of unique social nooks and niches. These encourage faculty, students, administrators and visitors to cross paths and mingle, allowing them to work and socialize in an environment that supports spontaneous interaction.

The building creates a new campus gateway, along with expanding and enhancing the outdoor courtyards that are a defining element of the Eastfield site. The gateway lobby includes a welcoming coffee kiosk/internet café to further promote the important social aspect of learning.

Adjacent conferencing facilities can be used after hours for both school and community activities. Brick veneer and plaster are the primary materials used for the building's exterior to provide consistency with the existing campus context. The Eastfield College Learning Center, which is a reinterpretation of iconic campus forms, will support and encourage lifelong learning for students of all interests.

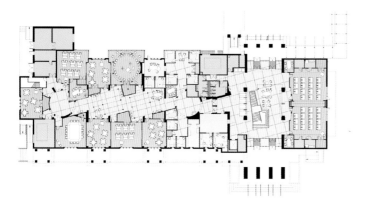

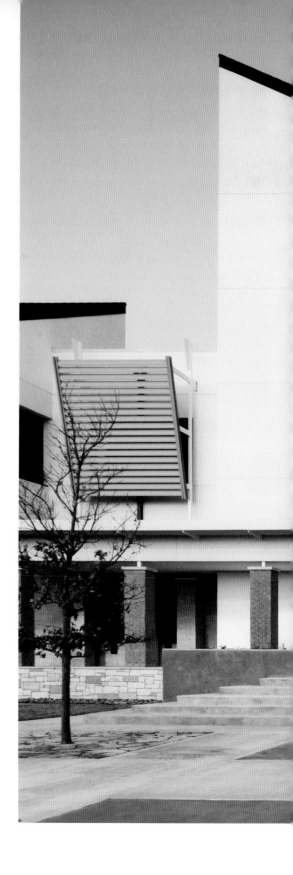

COMPREHENSIVE CANCER CENTER

Design/Completion:	2008
Location:	Wilmington, Delaware
Client:	confidential
Size:	440,000 square feet

This cancer center's design stemmed from the integration of water – the source of life, the simplest form of regeneration and growth – and the desire to provide contemporary and sustainable architecture that combine to encourage and stimulate interaction between doctors, patients, visitors and research scientists.

This comprehensive cancer center includes a 180-bed hospital, a clinic building and research labs on a 55-acre site while providing for parking and future growth.

A continuous reflecting pool fed from rooftop rainwater collection systems forms the main axis on the site, organizing the buildings and their relationship to one another. The pool starts at the hospital entry and flows downhill, connecting with the Delaware River. Bridges and walkways span the pools and connect the buildings, creating an informal public interaction space.

The orientation of each building maximizes views and celebrates existing vegetation and site conditions to create a natural sanctuary. Circulation paths between buildings become glass boxes that dematerialize and sit within the landscape.

The building materials promote healing, maximize natural daylighting and provide a modern and efficient design. The buildings will set the standard for sustainable and responsible design while serving as a beacon for cancer research, prevention and treatment.

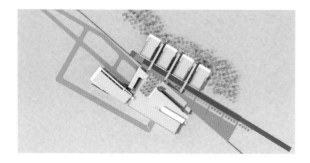

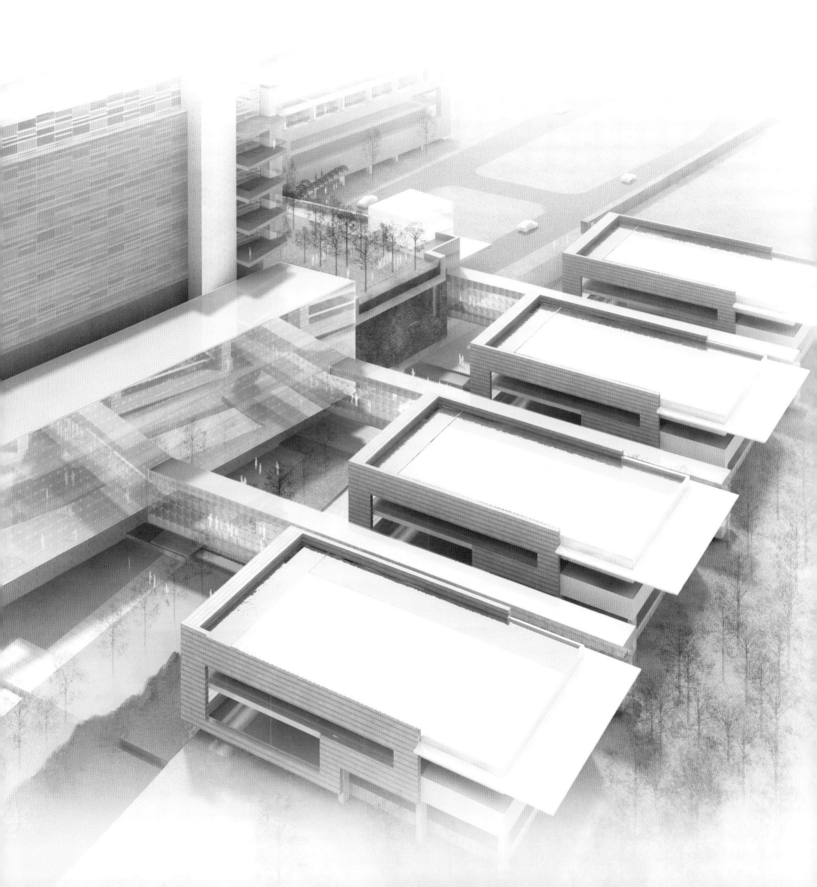

ERBIL IRAQ SCHOOLS

Design/Completion:	2005
Location:	Erbil, Iraq
Client:	Kurdistan Ministry of Education
Size:	190,000 square feet
Association:	Ryder HKS

The Kurdistan Ministry of Education, located in northern Iraq, believes the best way to improve living standards, political stability and personal security is to offer more and improved schooling opportunities. To meet this need, planning for six new schools on a single campus – including two kindergarten, two primary and two secondary schools – is underway by HKS in a venture with Mid-Atlantic Enterprises, Inc.

Developed to be one of the town's central meeting and gathering areas, the campus is arranged with a protective perimeter contributing to safety and security while thoughtfully offering a tree-lined avenue between the campus' outer façade and the adjacent apartment buildings.

Each school is comprised of standard classroom spaces clustered around common areas, which allow students and teachers to work inside and outside the traditional classroom environment. Reinforcing *tarbiyah* – the education and upbringing of the people – a place of worship is located at the center of the campus. Primary and secondary schools also feature communal areas for sporting activities. Featuring state-of-the-art international learning and instructional models adapted to local needs, the schools promote learning and a sense of community throughout Erbil.

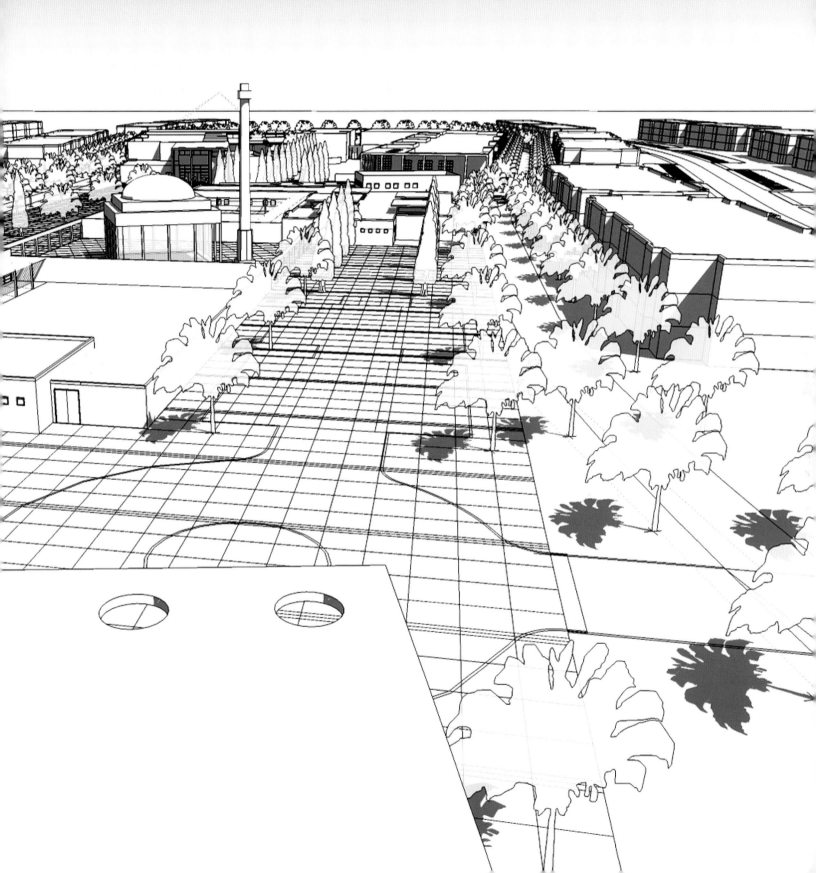

ACADEMIC TEACHING HOSPITAL

Design/Completion: 2011
Location: Middle East
Client: n/a
Size: 700,000 square feet

The overarching design premise for the academic teaching hospital is to shape a forward-thinking inpatient facility that thoughtfully responds to the context of the ancient city.

The tower concept is organized around four main principles including healing environment, connectivity, emergency medical response and sustainability. Functionally sound, adaptable and responsive to culturally diverse patient and family needs, the result is a design that consolidates all inpatient functions into one seamless and progressive building – while also establishing a new identity and main entrance to the campus.

Healing gardens and day rooms on each floor, a consolidated entrance atrium and a central vertical circulation spine that strategically separates the flow of materials, patients, visitors and staff between the units are all features of the building. The tower includes a consolidated logistics department, a full-service inpatient operating theatre and integrated sheltered facilities for emergency response situations. Patient-sensitive and environmentally responsible, the 450-bed tower is an innovative solution that provides a vital link between the past and future of the medical center.

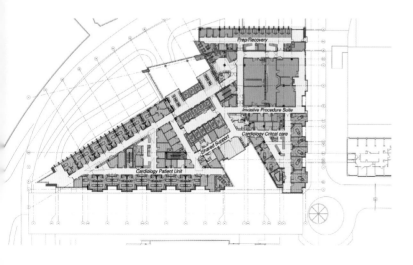

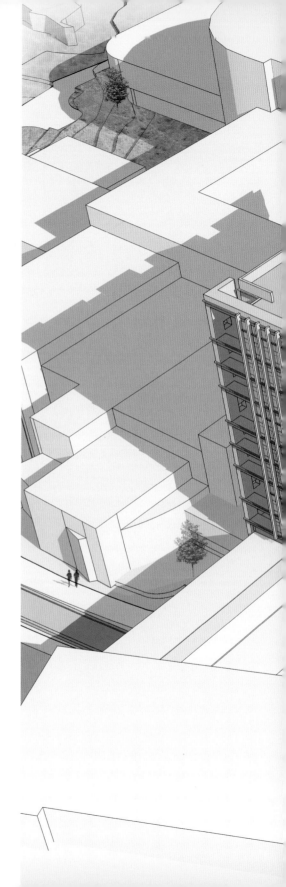

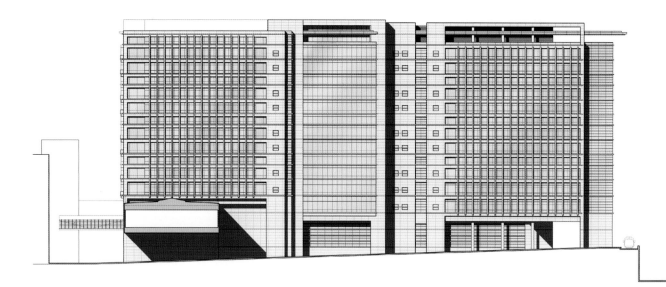

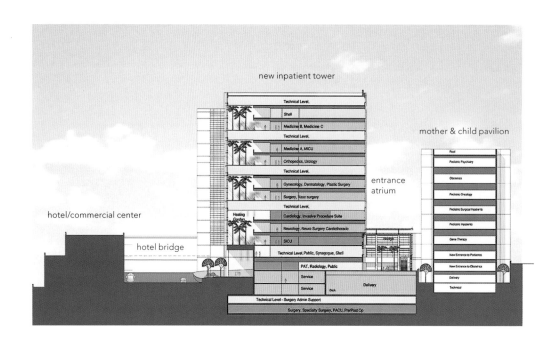

new inpatient tower

Technical Level,

Shell

Medicine B, Medicine C

Technical Level,

Medicine A, MICU

Orthopedics, Urology

Technical Level,

Gynecology, Dermatology, Plastic Surgery

Surgery, Vasc surgery

Technical Level,

Cardiology, Invasive Procedure Suite

Neurology, Neuro Surgery Cardiothoracic

SICU

Technical Level,Public, Synagogue, Shell

PAT, Radiology, Public

Service

Service

Technical Level - Surgery Admin Support

Surgery, Specialty Surgery, PACU, Pre/Post Op

mother & child pavilion

Roof

Pediatric Psychiatry

Obstetrics

Pediatric Oncology

Pediatric Surgical Inpatients

Pediatric Inpatients

Gene Therapy

New Entrance to Pediatrics

New Entrance to Obstetrics

Delivery

Technical

entrance atrium

Bridge

Healing Garden

hotel/commercial center

hotel bridge

Dock

Delivery

CHARLES E. SCHMIDT MEDICAL CENTER – MASTER PLAN

Design/Completion:	2007
Location:	Boca Raton, Florida
Client:	Boca Raton Community Hospital
Size:	1.1 million-square-foot academic medical center;
	150,000-square-foot medical office buildings

Recognizing the need to continue as a leader in providing safe, progressive healthcare and to better serve the community and surrounding areas, Boca Raton Community Hospital (BRCH) embarked upon an organizational restructuring and new facility plan – replacing an aging and near-obsolete facility built in 1965.

The organization's mission is to create the world's safest hospital. This master plan assists BRCH in directing the future of medical care with the addition of medical facilities at both of its southern and northern campuses, creating a medical corridor reaching out to the community.

A 100,000-square-foot comprehensive cancer center is the cornerstone of the southern campus expansion. The northern campus, located at Florida Atlantic University, provides more than 1 million square feet of inpatient care services, teaching facilities and physician office space.

The facility will be designed in conjunction with Florida Atlantic University (FAU) and the University of Miami (UM) to provide care to the Boca Raton community and surrounding areas as well as satisfy the teaching needs for the newly established medical school at FAU. The academic medical center creates a world-class facility that supports 21st-century healthcare delivered in a safe, family-friendly, patient-centered healing environment.

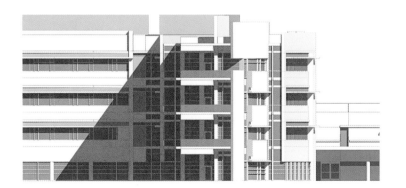

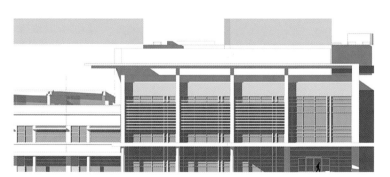

LEARN | CHARLES E. SCHMIDT MEDICAL CENTER – MASTER PLAN

THE COLLEGE OF NORTH WEST LONDON, WEMBLEY CAMPUS

Design/Completion:	2011
Location:	London, England
Client:	College of North West London
Size:	95,000 square feet

HKS Architects was appointed from stage A to develop designs for the College of North West London Wembley Park Centre for its submission to the Learning and Skills Council to deliver a facility to commence teaching in 2011.

The overall objective is to design and construct a high-quality, environmentally sustainable building for the college on a new site in Wembley. The site is a prime, high-profile location on a corner site adjoining Olympic Way and a busy road, opposite Wembley Park Underground Station and a short distance from Wembley Stadium. The site also spans a river, presenting a unique design challenge.

Facilities at the new building include hair and beauty salons, catering training kitchens and restaurant, specialist media suites and a multi-purpose black box performance space. The design solution features a transparent atrium space that showcases the activity within and acts as an advertisement for the college in the community.

The constrained footprint of the site has determined the eight-story form of the new building. This is mirrored by the vertical subject-based Learning Resource Centre, which allows each floor and specialist area to access information quickly and efficiently.

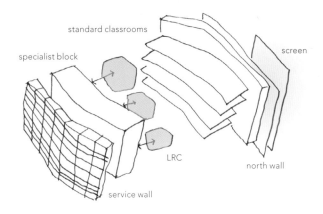

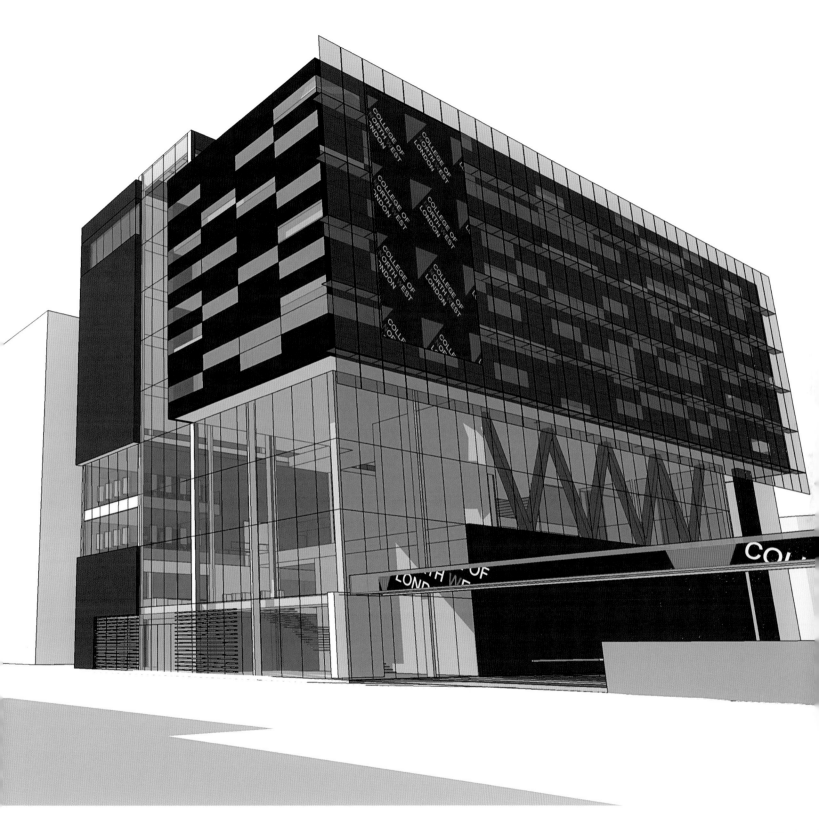

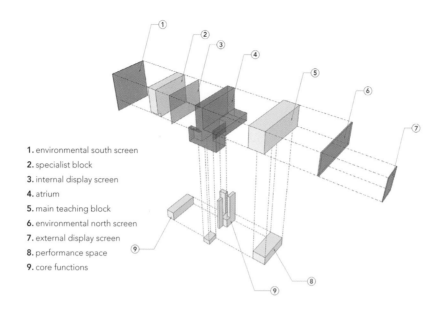

1. environmental south screen
2. specialist block
3. internal display screen
4. atrium
5. main teaching block
6. environmental north screen
7. external display screen
8. performance space
9. core functions

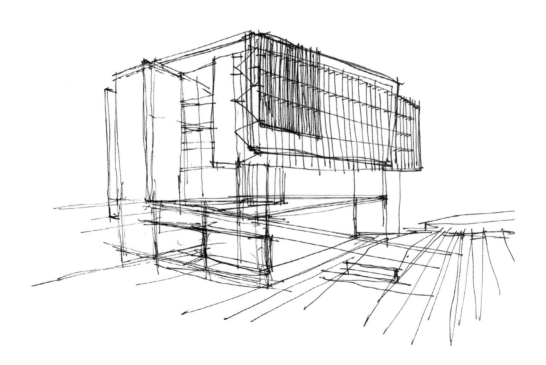

UK MEDICAL CENTRE FOR RESEARCH AND INNOVATION

Design/Completion:	2008
Location:	London, England
Client:	Medical Research Council, Cancer Research Council,
	University College Hospital and the Wellcome Trust
Size:	7 million square feet

A trend is emerging that is fueled by significant shifts in how the world chooses to work, how corporations define branding and what the next generation of workers expects in a workspace.

Those now entering the workforce attended schools where they sat at round tables rather than in rows, learned through collaborative projects rather than through individual assignments and used sophisticated technology to broaden and share their knowledge. These new employees are most drawn toward work environments that mirror that model. The corporate model lets companies take full advantage of flexible office systems that enable them to quickly and efficiently tailor their operational footprint as market conditions demand.

Shifts in how people work, where they would like to work and where they want to live suggest the corporate model will continue to evolve. As 21st-century employees increasingly define their office as "anytime, anywhere," architects will, in turn, design workspaces to serve more as connection points where face-to-face interactions occur rather than as cubicle clusters where tasks get processed.

HKS foresees the evolution of corporate design as an alignment of the cultures and strategic objectives of our corporate clients. This alignment transforms into architecture that will inspire productivity and innovation in future generations as well as achieve the ever-present need of real estate flexibility.

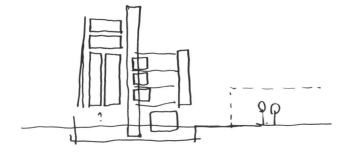

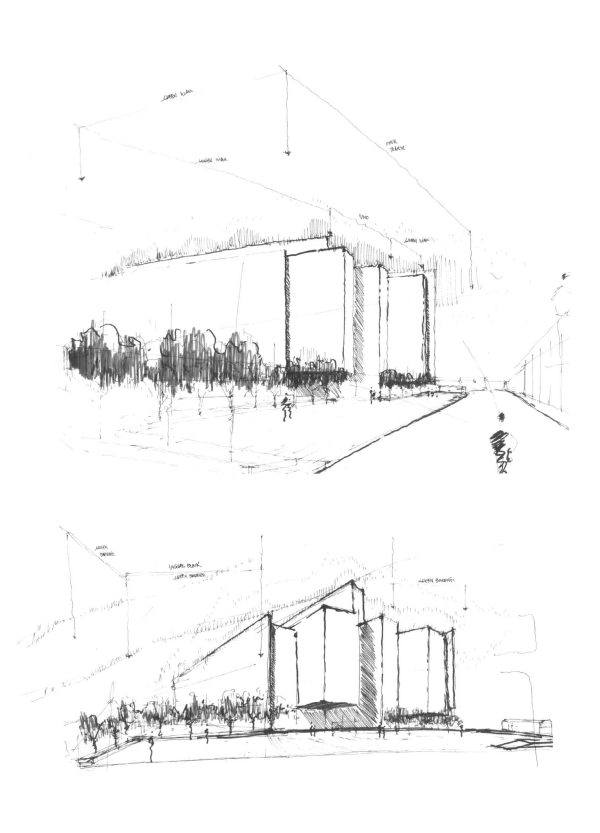

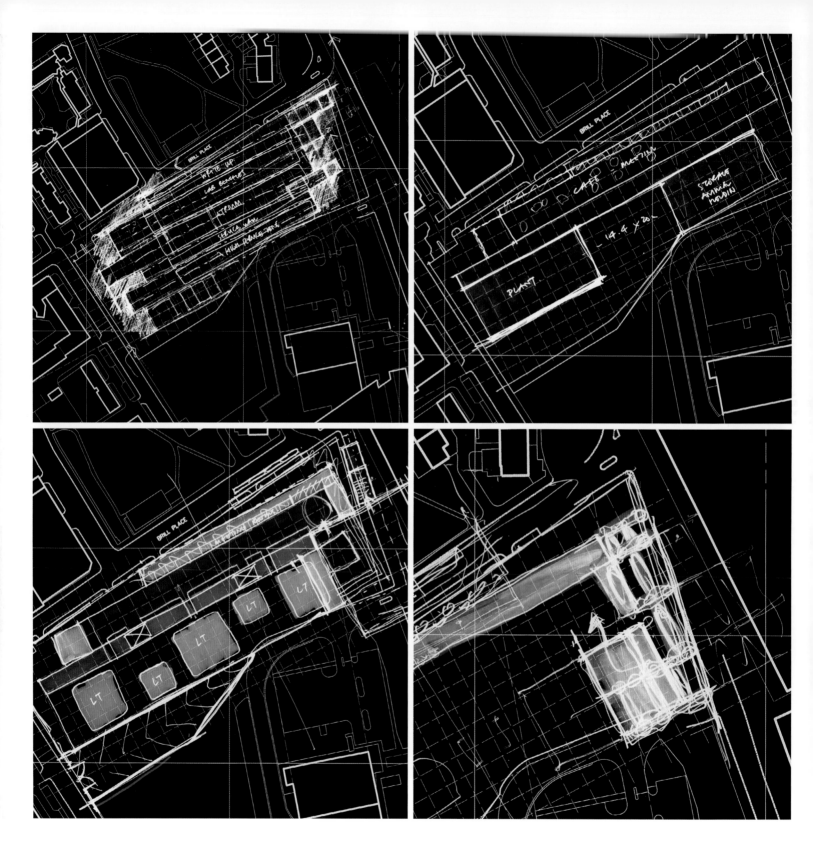

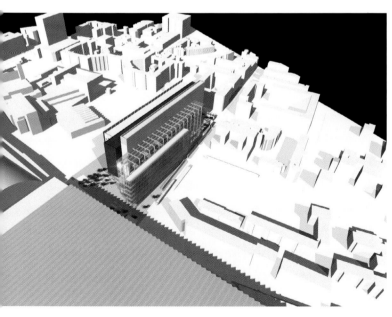

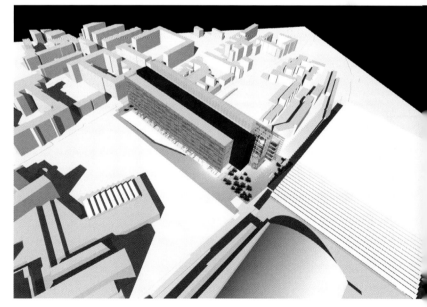

THE CENTER FOR AMERICAN AND INTERNATIONAL LAW

Design/Completion:	2001
Location:	Dallas, Texas
Client:	The Center for American and International Law
Size:	44,500 square feet

The Center for American and International Law represents the attributes of the legal system while providing the latest in education technology. The two-story facility, located on 7.5 acres, serves as both the center's administrative headquarters and an educational facility.

The facility is earmarked by a Jeffersonian-type dome. Natural warm hues of gray precast and French limestone plaster demonstrate the building's solid, timeless stature. Clear glass window walls extend a visual invitation of transparency that allowing views into the common areas and the landscaped quads of the complex.

A soothing water feature surrounds the circular entry while a 20- by 15-foot rounded corporate seal carved in French limestone adorns its west side. The Hall of Flags, with flags representing countries that have participated in the Center's programs, is visible from multiple levels in the main lobby.

Nine rooms, available for classes and meetings, range in capacity from 20 to 220 people. The Leon Jaworski and Charles W. Hall Courtroom hosts larger educational and related programs, the auditorium also hosts occasional court sessions and the Rogers Oil and Gas Room is used for special ceremonies and events.

The first floor houses teaching functions while the second story houses the center's executive area and law enforcement offices as well as accounting and support functions.

7 | LIVE

Bayway Lofts   328

Sonata   330

Press Telegram Lofts   332

Ten10   334

1000 Sunset Tower   336

BAYWAY LOFTS

Design/Completion: 2006
Location: St. Petersburg, Florida
Client: Grady Pridgen, Inc.
Size: 1 million square feet

Bayway Lofts allows residents to live, work and play in St. Petersburg's newest residences. Developing an iconic building based on nautical references was the design strategy. The project's overall massing and form evokes an image of an undulating glass sail. Additional design details also acknowledge the local context and nautical themes – sailing outriggers, the Sunshine Skyway Bridge and shell-like forms – executed in a contemporary fashion.

The two towers are oriented in an east–west direction on top of the podium to maximize views to Tampa Bay and the Gulf of Mexico. These towers incorporate a full-height glass skin, which provides unencumbered views for all of the residents. This undulating theme is also carried forward within a mural element for the parking garage screen, and in undulating paving bands of landscaping at the ground level.

Water features at the base of the buildings incorporate lighting that animates the lower levels of the towers at night with a texture of reflected water patterns.

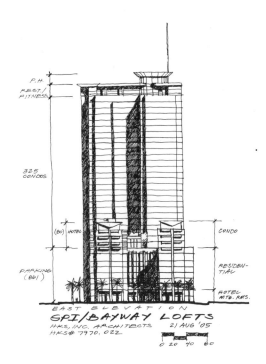

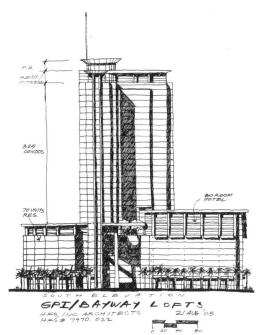

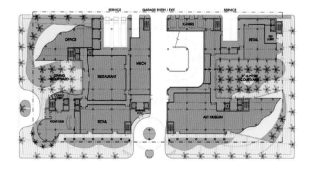

SONATA

Design/Completion: 2007
Location: St. Petersburg, Florida
Client: Grady Pridgen, Inc.
Size: 80,000-square-foot residential tower;
                      66,000-square-foot parking structure

Located on a 13,000-square-foot, mid-block downtown site adjacent to an alley with significant views to Tampa Bay and the Gulf of Mexico at the upper levels, this residential project derived its iconic expression by articulating each unit to create an overall architectural form. Code setback requirements necessitated a floor plate that stepped back from the parking podium, which yielded three units per floor, each unique in layout with multiple balconies to extend the spaces to the exterior. The multi-level penthouse suite meets the sky in a lantern-like form recalling nautical lighthouse references, while a ground-level retail arcade engages the urban fabric.

The building podium veils the parking from view on all sides, and contains a fully landscaped amenity deck level on top for the residents, which includes an outdoor lap pool with deck areas shaded by trellises. Internal amenities at this level contain a fitness center, media room, several meeting rooms and a wine room/dining area.

The exterior materials and colors were selected based on the nautical theme. Off-white precast concrete and granite accents at the building podium are extended up through the tower to encapsulate stair towers and mechanical areas, with pewter colored metal column covers and window wall accents providing additional sparkle in the sunlight. All balconies are clad with cantilevered glass balustrades, thereby maximizing the views to the water.

PRESS TELEGRAM LOFTS

Design/Completion:	2006
Location:	Long Beach, California
Client:	October 5 Development
Size:	560,000-square-foot residential space; 400,000-square-foot parking structure; 15,000-square-foot flexible space

Like many major Californian cities, Long Beach suffered a dramatic decline in affordable housing for essential members of the community – nurses, police officers, firefighters and teachers – who were forced to commute from the suburbs, increasing traffic, pollution and energy consumption.

The Press Telegram Lofts meets the needs of this underserved population. Located in the historic core of Long Beach, the 480-unit project mediates between the open, low-rise character of downtown and the density required to make middle-income housing a reality. In response to the pedestrian scale, the design meets the ground as a series of mid-rise structures, preserving the historic Press Telegram building and taking cues from the size and rhythm of its elements.

To prevent a monolithic appearance, each residential tower is split on its long axis into a solid and a glassy component, each of which slides a half bay to emphasize the difference. From a distance, this change distinguishes the towers from one another, and the glass further dematerializes the buildings in the maritime sky. The top of the podium is the social heart of the building, with community rooms, landscaped areas and a pool in the sunlit southern portion of the deck.

TEN10

Design/Completion:	2007
Location:	Los Angeles, California
Client:	Lennar Urban, First United Methodist Church
Size:	417,000 square feet

Ten10 melds two distinctly different impulses: the service-oriented mission of the First United Methodist Church of Los Angeles and the financial requirements of a private developer. By expressing the diversity of Los Angeles culture, the program of a community-based church and iconography from strong Protestant tradition, the design reconciles these disparate goals.

The church has long been a home for community organizations, reaching out to the less fortunate. To enhance this connection, the new sanctuary is placed at ground level, with operable panels leading directly to a pocket park on the street.

Inside, stadium seating provides congregation members with a direct view of the street scene. A sky chapel on top of the podium provides a quiet refuge for special occasions. Its metallic fish-like shape, lined on the interior with wood, is evocative of the early calling of Jesus of Nazareth, while embracing the provocative formal language characteristic of modern Los Angeles architecture.

The tower comprises several distinct elements: a precast façade reminiscent of I Ching diagrams, a metallic veil shielding the west elevation and a north-facing glassy block defined by shaped balconies that subtly trace the outline of the Methodist Church's primary symbol – the flame-enshrouded cross.

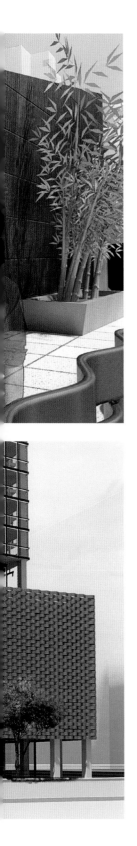

1000 SUNSET TOWER

Design/Completion:	2009
Location:	Los Angeles, California
Client:	EP&C Equity Trust
Size:	756,000 square feet

1000 Sunset is poised to be Los Angeles' next landmark mixed-used development. Located near the heart of downtown at the intersection of the 110 and 101 freeways, 1000 Sunset will serve as the eastern anchor of legendary Sunset Boulevard. This premier 36-story tower features 15 levels of office lease space, nine levels of high-end condominiums, a roof deck and garden, a sky lobby and ground-level retail. 1000 Sunset offers residents and tenants the convenience of freeway access as well as an address that demands attention.

Overlooking the city, 1000 Sunset offers sweeping unimpeded views stretching from downtown Los Angeles to the Hollywood Hills to the Pacific Ocean. 1000 Sunset's design embodies the essence of Los Angeles: a vibrant and adventurous setting, quilted together by myriad eclectic and distinct communities and industries. The segmented glass façade becomes a reflection of that energy. Throughout the day, each segment of the façade reflects a unique element of the city, creating a diverse image on the tower's façade.

At the base of the tower, segmented vertical gardens tie the building to the ground and reference the community's promise to make Los Angeles a green city. This development epitomizes the energy of the city, never before realized in a building of its stature. This is truly desirable and distinct living for the environmentally committed citizens of Los Angeles.

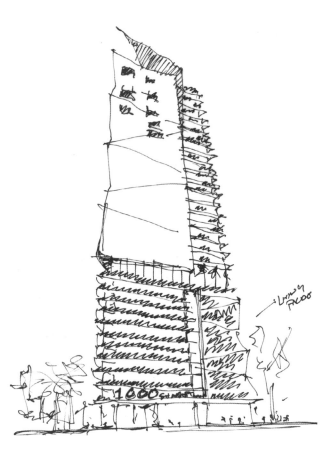

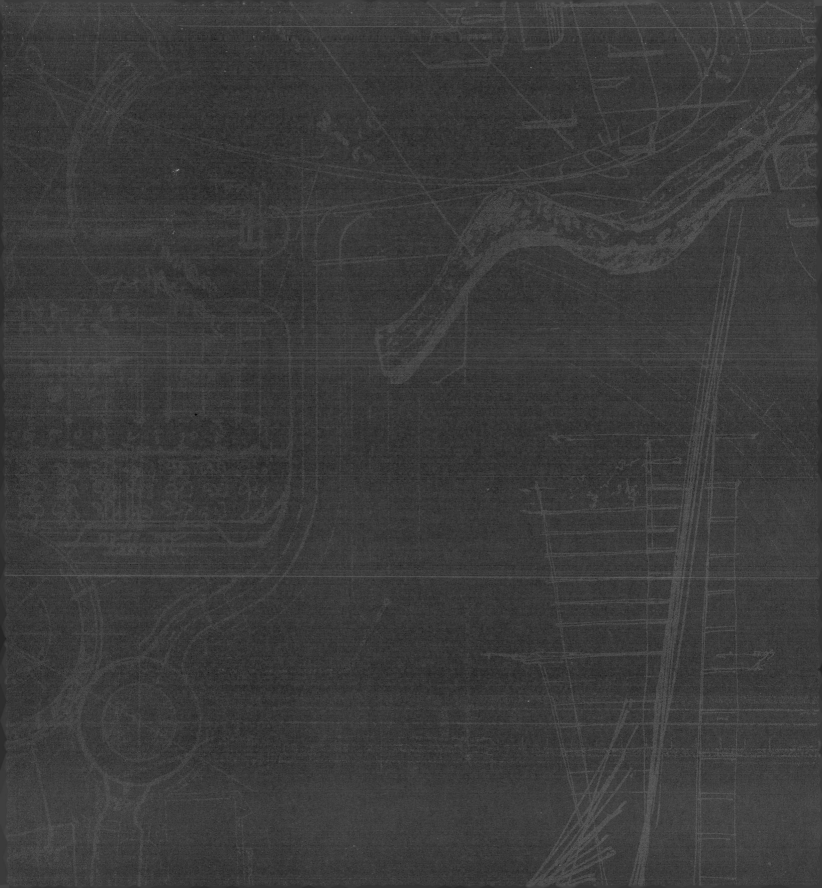

8 | STUDY

2006 HKS Design Fellowship Museum Tower   342

2007 HKS Design Fellowship   344

2008 HKS Design Fellowship   346

Land_Scraper   348

West End Pedestrian Bridge   350

National Museum of Art, Architecture and Design 352

Statler Competition "A Temporary Façade"   354

2006 HKS DESIGN FELLOWSHIP MUSEUM TOWER

Design/Completion: 2006

Location: Dallas, Texas

Client: HKS, Inc.

Size: n/a

The Museum Tower was developed in conjunction with the Woodall Rodgers Deck
Park to knit four disparate districts in the downtown Dallas area into a cohesive
whole. In addition, a powerful east–west link was created to orient both pedestrian and vehicular traffic while linking the Dallas Arts District, the West End
and Uptown.

The solution creates a highly sculptural building that responds to both downtown,
with its vertical architectural expression, and the deck park that follows a more
linear, horizontal vocabulary. The tower draws from downtown's straight-edged
city grid expressing it with angles that mimic the streets and cantilevers that offer
unobstructed views.

Generous covered terraces at key points create a visual connection with the Arts
District, allowing residents to feel as if they can bring a piece of the park into
their condo. Crisp, clean edges form a jewel case made from exposed concrete
that contains and protects the golden-orange stained glass – recalling how the
museum showcases and protects invaluable art collections. Artwork in its own
right, the building will glow at night, creating a beacon toward the livelihood of
the deck park. This graceful response symbolizes unity, blurring the lines between
architecture and art and merging them in a common gesture.

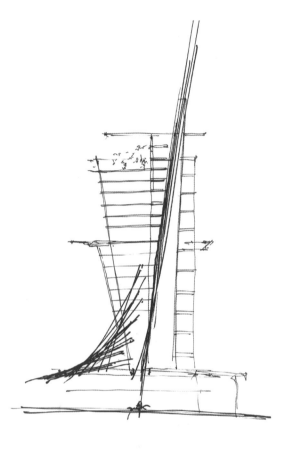

2007 HKS DESIGN FELLOWSHIP

Design/Completion:	2007
Location:	Oak Cliff, Texas
Client:	HKS, Inc.
Size:	n/a

REACH is the conceptual result of a series of ideas developed through the investigation process of the potential of the Oak Cliff site. At its core, the concept attempts to define a relationship of the duality inherent in water while redefining a lost connection between the river and its people. The solution exposes physical and socio-economic dualities and provides one solution to breaching the divide between nature versus culture and economy versus humanity.

The levee's impact is reduced by using a majority of the site as a gently sloping connector park between the city and the river. A physical breach of the levee reverses the gentle slope to the inside of the levee, creating an amphitheater. This juxtaposition of slopes allows visitors to gently climb over the levee and access the Trinity River. In addition, a library, a mixed-use tower, and parking for residents and visitors are carefully planned to minimize the obstruction of the stunning views toward downtown for visitors and neighbors while maximizing the availability of the park to all residents. The breach of the levee, therefore, is a gesture that breaks apart the barrier and reunites the city to the river economically, physically and theoretically.

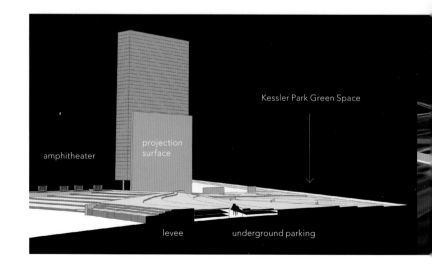

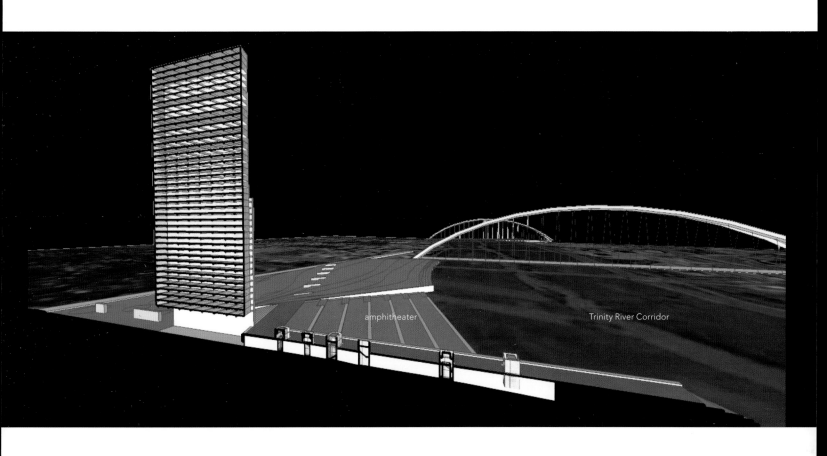

amphitheater

Trinity River Corridor

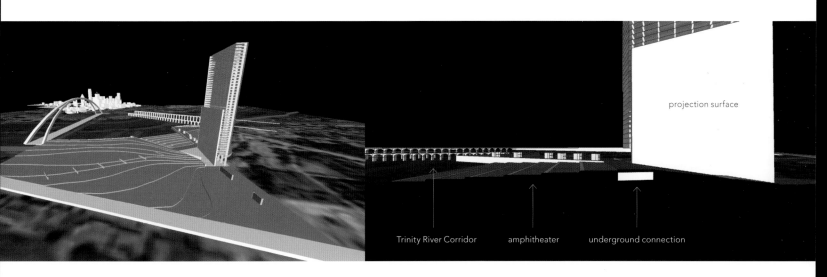

projection surface

Trinity River Corridor   amphitheater   underground connection

2008 HKS DESIGN FELLOWSHIP

Design/Completion:	2008
Location:	Dallas, Texas
Client:	HKS, Inc.
Size:	n/a

Lying outside the freeways encircling Dallas, this site on the edge of Deep Ellum is disconnected from downtown's corporate edifices by the raised highway I-75. The two districts create a tension; the site lies in a zone of friction and becomes a place of transition.

Dallas' two dominant planning grids clash on the site to create a geometric framework that changes in scale throughout the site, into which forms are defined, expressed and ordered. The transition in scale from downtown into Deep Ellum informs the sectional organization.

A diverse array of functions extend to the local community and provide 24-hour support for office workers; from hotels with a gallery lobby to a car park within a park; from coffee/book shops to gyms and dance studios; from screening rooms and concert venues to food markets, condos and a global architecture practice. The architectural office becomes the transitioning piece of the arrangement, mitigating the transition from the cultural influences and creativity of the Deep Ellum District to the company's global presence.

The building's skin becomes digital graffiti, recalling the much-loved, defunct Deep Ellum graffiti tunnel. As the office touches the streetscape, the glazed galley arena displays architecture in process; design reviews, displays and exhibitions become street graffiti – a stage for transition.

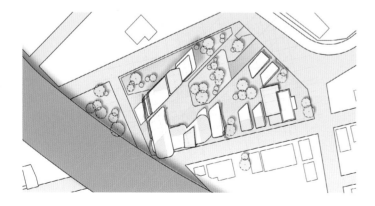

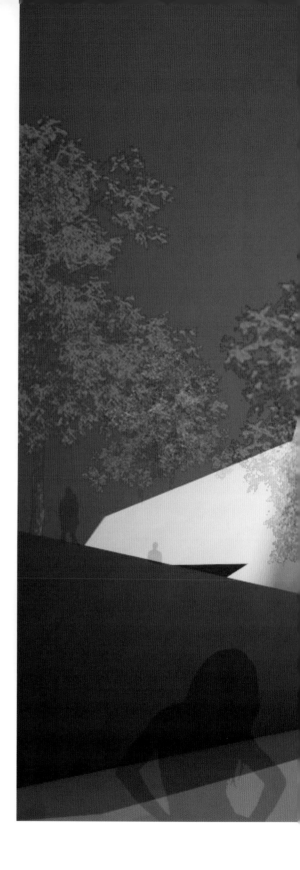

LAND_SCRAPER

Design/Completion:	2009
Location:	Dallas, Texas
Client:	eVolo International Skyscraper Competition
Size:	13 million square feet

Land_Scraper is an overturned vertical skyscraper, rescaled toward the human experience. Spanning more than 1,500 feet and five city blocks, the building winds through three districts including the Performing Arts District, the east side of the Financial District and the residential sector of historic Deep Ellum.

This project seeks a balance within its neighborhoods, encouraging more pedestrian and public experiences throughout the day and night. As the surface deviates to interact with each district, a relationship occurs that expresses the importance of each sector. Business in the center becomes the less meaningful sector, allowing pedestrians to ascend above. Residential and performing arts sectors are more embracing of the urban context.

Land_Scraper is designed with the notion of rethinking circulation and connectivity within a dense urban fabric. The horizontality creates a greater sense of scale and fluidity for the user in a primarily vertical atmosphere.

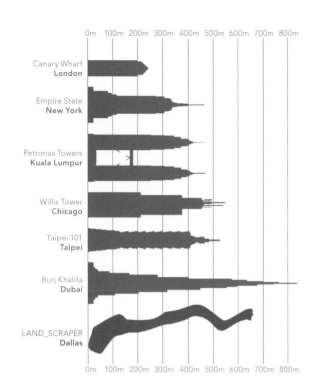

section AA   section BB   section CC

■ retail
■ arts
■ commercial
■ living
  public

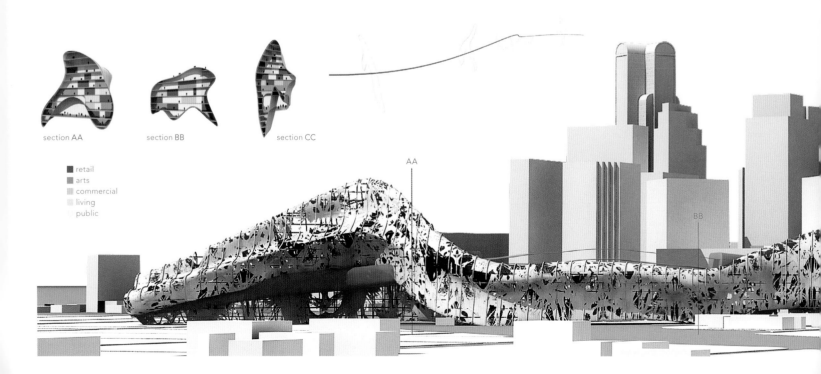

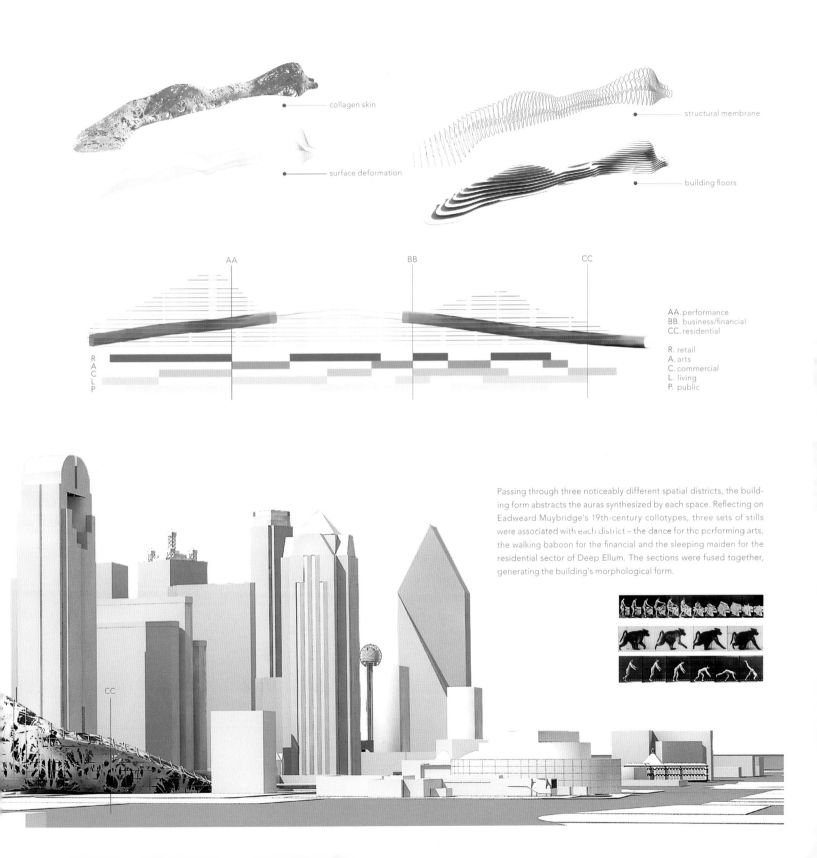

collagen skin

surface deformation

structural membrane

building floors

AA
BB
CC

AA. performance
BB. business/financial
CC. residential

R. retail
A. arts
C. commercial
L. living
P. public

R
A
C
L
P

Passing through three noticeably different spatial districts, the building form abstracts the auras synthesized by each space. Reflecting on Eadweard Muybridge's 19th-century collotypes, three sets of stills were associated with each district – the dance for the performing arts, the walking baboon for the financial and the sleeping maiden for the residential sector of Deep Ellum. The sections were fused together, generating the building's morphological form.

CC

WEST END PEDESTRIAN BRIDGE

Design/Completion: 2006
Location: Pittsburgh, Pennsylvania
Client: Riverlife Task Force
Size: n/a

The West End Pedestrian Bridge addition is a celebration of the historic city of Pittsburgh. The bridge provides a destination and connection, framing and enhancing exhilarating views of the hills, river and skyline while promoting human interaction and paying tribute to the city's long-standing symbols.

The project observes the history of bridges along the riverfront while maintaining integrity and respect for the existing West End Bridge. The new bridge connects neighboring communities and builds on the distinguished history of these unique landmarks.

The project honors its connection with the original bridge through a design that pays homage by sharing structural roles, yet expands its gracefulness by cantilevering out in a daring way, establishing the differences in structural technologies that span 80 years.

The design strikes a balance between old and new – embracing the clean and elegant lines of its predecessor while creating a visually exciting yet simple style. Its lines depart from the symmetrical approach and solidity of yesterday and into the daring off-centered lines that provide ever-changing views to be experienced from different perspectives.

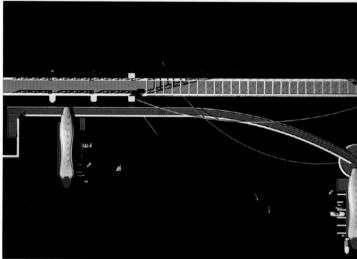

NATIONAL MUSEUM OF ART, ARCHITECTURE AND DESIGN

Design/Completion:	2009
Location:	Oslo, Norway
Client:	Ministry of Culture and Church Affairs, Norway
Size:	98,000 square feet

STÅCKVÅULTJENGÅ, the design for the National Museum of Art, Architecture and Design in Oslo, stacks and propels the art storage vault spaces into the exhibit spaces, inviting visitors and staff to experience the museum's cultural and historical depth and significance. The art storage vaults serve as structure, partition and, at times, exhibition space for the innermost workings of the museum's operations. The project program required diverse spaces – including exhibition spaces for temporary exhibition, contemporary art, older art, furniture and textiles. The corresponding vaults store 75 percent of their collection, forming the initial concept for the architectural expression.

In the same way that the art storage vaults allow glimpses into the museum's operations, the building's skin allows views and light to filter through the carefully planned joinery between the heavy stones that create the building's skin. The museum reveals itself and its contents with multiple, conceptual layers.

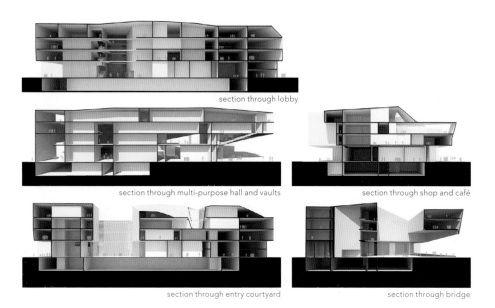

section through lobby

section through multi-purpose hall and vaults

section through shop and café

section through entry courtyard

section through bridge

Wh/m2

600+
580
560
540
520
500
480
460
440
420
400

A TYPICAL EXTERIOR WALL SYSTEM DEVELOPED FROM A SOLAR
ACCESS ANALYSIS CALCULATION.

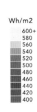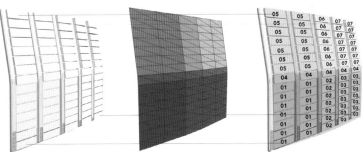

Stone wall system of
various depths for increased
radiant control.

Total radiation analysis
(Wh/m2) at cumulated
date and time.

Overlay model showing
proportional stone sizes based
on thermal intensity levels.

STATLER COMPETITION
"A TEMPORARY FAÇADE"

Design/Completion:	2010
Location:	Dallas, Texas
Client:	AIA Dallas
Size:	n/a

Constructed in 1956, the Dallas Statler Hotel is a mid-century architectural icon. Unfortunately, this nationally registered landmark has been vacant since 2001, and currently is looking for a redefinition of its image. The city is in the process of developing a collection of housing in uptown Dallas and cultural hotspots such as the Arts District. However, the Statler Hotel is choosing to revitalize existing urban vacancies and infrastructure instead of demolishing and building new.

This proposal intends to be a temporal stimulus of activity in the area. In studying the context, several programmatic decisions were made that would almost immediately increase the density and activity in the area, from nomadic vendors to exhibition spaces. Once the park adjacent to the Statler Hotel is complete, this area should begin to generate new life and interaction with this design.

An in-depth study produced a diversity chart of buildings and their uses in a quarter-mile radius around the site. It was determined that the lack of urban program diversity and people are two primary reasons why the area is vacant. That program driver was used to begin mapping the skin as a voided element and projection. This began a clear understanding of the services and functions that would occupy the sectors of Statler's façade. These functions include newspaper stands, trash/recycle bins, vending, bus stops, musical venues and art exhibitions.

These nested typologies will transform their functional profiles to correspond to the live, work and play environment. Material conservation will be a priority by using recycled and reclaimed wood, metal shards, plastics and fabrics from local construction sites and factories. The final process will reuse the structural framing for park amenities such as overhangs, sculptures and temporary weathering shelters.

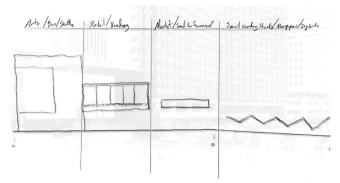

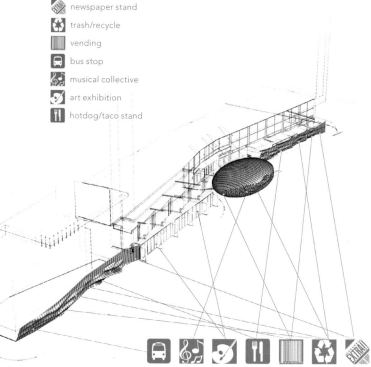

newspaper stand
trash/recycle
vending
bus stop
musical collective
art exhibition
hotdog/taco stand

Programmatic components that make up the façade, each in relation to the park and the urban context.

9 | APPENDIX

Design Awards 2000–2009	358
Firm Awards 2000–2009	366
Photography Credits	367
Index	368

DESIGN AWARDS 2000–2009

Baptist Health Medical Center – North Little Rock
North Little Rock, Arkansas
Merit Award, 2000 (American Institute of Architects/Arkansas Chapter)

Citibank Center – Tampa
Tampa, Florida
Excellence Award, 2000 (Architectural Precast Association)

Citibank Center – Tampa
Tampa, Florida
Excellence Award, 2000 (Tampa Bay Regional Planning Council)

Dell Diamond Ballpark
Round Rock (Austin), Texas
Best New Ballpark, 2000 (Ballparks.com)

DFW International Airport Terminal D
Dallas/Fort Worth, Texas
Award of Merit – Conceptual/Unbuilt, 2000 (American Institute of Architects/Northern Virginia Chapter)

DFW International Airport Terminal D
Dallas/Fort Worth, Texas
Citation Award Unbuilt, 2000 (American Institute of Architects/Dallas Chapter)

Hackensack University Medical Office Building
Hackensack, New Jersey
Merit Award, 2000 (New Jersey Concrete and Aggregate Association)

Lincoln Plaza at SunTrust Center*
Orlando, Florida
Award of Excellence/Golden Brick, 2000 (Downtown Orlando Partnership)

M.D. Anderson Cancer Center*
Houston, Texas
Scientific Institutes/Design Solutions Magazine Award, 2000 (American Woodwork Institute)

Performing Arts Rehearsal Hall*
Fort Worth, Texas
Golden Trowel Award of Excellence, 2000 (United Masonry Contractors Association)

Shutts & Bowen, LLP
Orlando Florida
Award of Excellence/Golden Brick, 2000 (Downtown Orlando Partnership)

Washoe Village Care Center*
Reno, Nevada
Design for Aging Review Award, 2000 (American Institute of Architects)

Westlake Corporate Campus
Westlake, Texas
Merit Award, 2000 (American Institute of Architects/Arkansas Chapter)

American Airlines Center*
Dallas, Texas
Best New Major Venue Award, 2001 (Concert Industry Consortium)

American Airlines Center*
Dallas, Texas
Best of 2001 Judges Award, 2001 (F.W. Dodge)

American Airlines Center*
Dallas, Texas
Golden Trowel Award of Excellence, 2001 (United Masonry Contractors Association)

American Airlines Center*
Dallas, Texas
Honor Award, 2001 (The National Terrazzo & Mosaic Association)

American Airlines Center*
Dallas, Texas
International Excellence in Masonry Award, 2001 (Masonry Contractors Association of America)

American Airlines Center*
Dallas, Texas
Mega Project Over $100 Million, 2001 (Associated Builders and Contractors)

American Airlines Center*
Dallas, Texas
Minority Business Development Agency Outstanding Corporate Award, 2001 (United States Department of Commerce)

American Airlines Center*
Dallas, Texas
Outstanding Project Over $25 Million, 2001 (American Subcontractor Association)

American Airlines Center*
Dallas, Texas
Outstanding Project Team of the Year, 2001 (American Subcontractor Association)

American Airlines Center*
Dallas, Texas
Phoenix Award, 2001 (United States EPA)

Bob Bullock State History Museum*
Austin, Texas
$25 to $99 Million Institutional Category Award, 2001 (North Texas Associated Builders and Contractors, Inc.)

Bob Bullock State History Museum*

Austin, Texas

Job of the Year, 2001 (The National Terrazzo & Mosaic Association)

Dell Diamond Ballpark

Round Rock (Austin), Texas

Architectural Showcase Award, 2001 (Athletic Business)

Dell Diamond Ballpark

Round Rock (Austin), Texas

Excellence in Construction Award, 2001 (Associated General Contractors of America/Austin Chapter)

Dr Pepper StarsCenter

Euless, Texas

Summit Award, 2001 (Associated General Contractors of America/Dallas Chapter)

Jones Day

Dallas, Texas

Merit Award, 2001 (IIDA Texas/Oklahoma Chapter)

Miller Park*

Milwaukee, Wisconsin

Concrete Design Award, 2001 (Wisconsin Ready Mixed Concrete Association)

Utah Valley Regional Medical Center Women's and Children's Addition

Provo, Utah

Healthcare Design Award, 2001 (The Center for Health Design)

Washoe Village Care Center*

Reno, Nevada

Design for Aging Review Award, 2001 (American Institute of Architects)

American Airlines Center*

Dallas, Texas

Engineering Excellence Award, 2002 (American Council of Engineering Companies)

American Airlines Center*

Dallas, Texas

Facility of Merit, 2002 (Athletic Business)

American Airlines Center*

Dallas, Texas

Minority Business Development Agency Outstanding Corporate Award, 2002 (United States Department of Commerce)

American Airlines Center*

Dallas, Texas

Project of the Year Award, 2002 (Masonry Construction)

American Airlines Center*

Dallas, Texas

QUOIN Award, 2002 (Associated General Contractors of America/Dallas/Fort Worth Chapter)

American Airlines Center*

Dallas, Texas

Real Estate Deals Award, 2002 (Dallas Business Journal)

Bank One Building

Fort Worth, Texas

National Design Excellence Award, 2002 (Cast Stone Institute)

Bob Bullock State History Museum*

Austin, Texas

Award of Excellence, 2002 (Austin Commercial Real Estate Society)

JP Morgan International Plaza I & II

Farmers Branch, Texas

Project of the Year Award, 2002 (Dallas Business Journal)

Lincoln Park II

Tysons Corner, Virginia

Award of Excellence, 2002 (Northern Virginia National Association of Industrial and Office Properties)

Methodist Medical Center Inpatient Surgical Suite Renovation

Dallas, Texas

Award of Merit, 2002 (Texas Construction)

Methodist Medical Center Surgery Renovation

Dallas, Texas

ABC Excellence in Construction, First Place, 2002 (Associated General Contractors of America/Dallas Chapter)

Obici Hospital

Suffolk, Virginia

Golden Trowel Award of Excellence, 2002 (United Masonry Contractors Association)

Obici Hospital

Suffolk, Virginia

Honor Award, 2002 (Illumination Engineering Society of North America)

University of North Carolina Children's Hospital University of North Carolina Women's Hospital

Chapel Hill, North Carolina

Honor Award, 2002 (National Terrazzo & Mosaic Association)

West Texas A&M University Event Center
Amarillo, Texas
Excellence in Construction Award, 2002
(Associated Builders and Contractors)

Westin at Times Square*
New York, New York
Hospitality Project of the Year, 2002 (New York
Construction News)

Baptist Health Medical Center – North Little Rock
North Little Rock, Arkansas
Citation of Excellence, 2003 (American Institute of
Architects Architecture for Health Facilities Review)

Dr Pepper/7 Up Ballpark
Frisco, Texas
Award for Excellence, 2003 (Society of American
Registered Architects)

Dr Pepper/7 Up Ballpark
Frisco, Texas
Merit Award, 2003 (American Institute of
Architects/Fort Worth Chapter)

Emory Crawford Long Hospital
Atlanta, Georgia
Large Scale Project of the Year Award, 2003
(Urban Land Institute's Atlanta Chapter)

McKinney Avenue Lofts
Dallas, Texas
Golden Trowel Award of Excellence, 2003
(United Masonry Contractors Association)

Miller Park*
Milwaukee, Wisconsin
Design and Manufacturing Excellence Award,
2003 (Architectural Precast Association)

Nancy Lee & Perry R. Bass Performing Arts Center*
Fort Worth, Texas
Merit Award, 2003 (American Institute of Architects/
Fort Worth Chapter)

Obici Hospital
Suffolk, Virginia
Award of Merit, 2003 (American Institute of Architects
Architecture for Health Facilities Review)

Obici Hospital
Suffolk, Virginia
Illumination Design Award, 2003 (National Terrazzo
& Mosaic Association)

Obici Hospital
Suffolk, Virginia
Merit Award of Excellence, 2003 (James River Virginia AIA)

Obici Hospital
Suffolk, Virginia
Vista Award, Honorable Mention, 2003 (American Institute
of Architect's Academy of Architecture for Health)

Parker Adventist Hospital
Parker, Colorado
Symposium Distinction Award, 2003 (Symposium
on Healthcare Design)

Phoenix Sky Harbor Rental Care Center*
Phoenix, Arizona
Merit Award, 2003 (San Mateo County California
American Institute of Architects)

Seuss Landing
Orlando, Florida
Award of Merit, Project $25 million or greater, 2003
(American Institute of Steel Construction)

St. Rose Dominican Hospital – Siena Campus
Henderson, Nevada
Symposium Distinction Award, 2003 (Symposium
on Healthcare Design)

Sterling Commerce
Irving, Texas
TOBY Award/Office Building of the Year, 2003 (Building
Owners and Managers Association of America [BOMA])

The Dallas Convention Center – 2002 Expansion*
Dallas, Texas
Award of Merit, Project $100 million or greater, 2003
(American Institute of Steel Construction)

The George Washington University Hospital
Washington, D.C.
Excellence in Construction Award, 2003 (Associated
Builders and Contractors)

American Airlines Center*
Dallas, Texas
Topping Out Award, 2004 (Dallas Business Journal)

Baptist Health Medical Center – North Little Rock
North Little Rock, Arkansas
Design Citation, New Hospital Category, 2004
(AIA Academy of Architecture for Health)

Baylor Medical Plaza Parking Structure
Baylor University Medical Center
Dallas, Texas
Award of Excellence, 2004 (Prestressed
Concrete Institute)

Children's Medical Center of Dallas
Dallas, Texas
Topping Out Award, 2004 (Dallas Business Journal)

Exempla Good Samaritan Medical Center
Lafayette, Colorado
Gold Hard Hat Award, 2004 (Colorado Construction)

Frost Bank Tower
Austin, Texas
Impact Award for Design Excellence, 2004
(Downtown Austin Alliance)

Obici Hospital
Suffolk, Virginia
Design Citation, New Hospital Category, 2004
(AIA Academy of Architecture for Health)

Orlando Public Library
Orlando, Florida
Honor in Architecture, 2004 (AIA Orlando Chapter)

Parker Adventist Hospital
Parker, Colorado
Gold Hard Hat Award, 2004 (Colorado Construction)

Parker Adventist Hospital
Parker, Colorado
Healthcare Design Citation of Merit, 2004
(The Center for Health Design)

Parker Adventist Hospital
Parker, Colorado
Symposium Distinction Award, 2004 (Symposium
on Healthcare Design)

Parker Adventist Hospital
Parker, Colorado
The Award of Excellence, 2004 (AIA Modern Healthcare
Design Competition)

Pinellas County Medical Examiners and
Forensics Center
Largo, Florida
Architecture for Justice Knowledge Community –
Justice Facilities Review, 2004 (American Institute
of Architects)

Sabre Headquarters
Southlake, Texas
Topping Out Award, 2004 (Dallas Business Journal)

Sterling Commerce
Irving, Texas
TOBY Award/Office Building of the Year, 2004 (Building
Owners and Managers Association of America [BOMA])

The Dallas Convention Center – 2002 Expansion*
Dallas, Texas
Topping Out Award, 2004 (Dallas Business Journal)

Watermark Hotel and Spa
San Antonio, Texas
Gold Key Award for Excellence, 2004 (Hotels and
Interior Design)

Washington Regional Medical Center
Fayetteville, Arkansas
Healthcare Design Award, 2004 (The Center for
Health Design)

Watermark Hotel and Spa
San Antonio, Texas
Golden Trowel Award of Excellence, 2004
(United Masonry Contractors Association)

Westlake Corporate Campus
Westlake, Texas
Topping Out Award, 2004 (Dallas Business Journal)

Abbott Northwestern Heart Hospital
Minneapolis, Minnesota
Symposium Distinction User-Centered Award,
2005 (Symposium on Healthcare Design)

Seattle Children's Hospital
Seattle, Washington
Healthcare Design Award, 2005 (The Center for
Health Design)

Seattle Children's Hospital
Seattle, Washington
Symposium Distinction Team Award, 2005 (Symposium
on Healthcare Design)

Seattle Children's Hospital
Seattle, Washington
VISTA Award, 2005 (American Institute of Architects'
Academy of Architecture for Health)

Clarian North Medical Center
Carmel, Indiana
Carmel Look Award, 2005 (Carmel Chamber of Commerce)

DFW International Airport Terminal D
Dallas/Fort Worth, Texas
Access Award, 2005 (American Foundation for the Blind)

DFW International Airport Terminal D
Dallas/Fort Worth, Texas
Excellence in Diversity Award, 2005 (Dallas/Fort Worth's
Small & Emerging Business Development)

DFW International Airport Terminal D
Dallas/Fort Worth, Texas
Innovator Award, 2005 (Dallas Mayor's Committee
for the Employment of People with Disabilities)

DFW International Airport Terminal D
Dallas/Fort Worth, Texas
Topping Out Award, 2005 (Dallas Business Journal)

Dr Pepper/7 Up Ballpark
Frisco, Texas
Best New Ballpark, 2005 (Ballparks.com)

Dr Pepper/7 Up Ballpark
Frisco, Texas
Topping Out Award, 2005 (Dallas Business Journal)

Garland Special Events Center
Garland, Texas
Design Award, 2005 (Texas Association of School
Boards/Texas Association of School Administrators)

Grand Prairie ISD Gopher-Warrior Bowl
Grand Prairie, Texas
Project of Distinction, 2005 (Education Design
Showcase, School Planning and Management)

Emory Crawford Long Hospital
Atlanta, Georgia
Healthcare Design Award, 2005 (The Center for Health Design)

JP Morgan International Plaza I & II
Farmers Branch, Texas
*TOBY Award/Office Building of the Year, 2005 (Building
Owners and Managers Association of America [BOMA])*

M-E Engineers
Culver City, California
Interiors Award, 2005 (Contract)

Millennium Center
Addison, Texas
*Southwest Region Award, 2005 (Building Owners and
Managers Association of America [BOMA])*

Millennium Center
Addison, Texas
*TOBY Award/Office Building of the Year, 2005 (Building
Owners and Managers Association of America [BOMA])*

Parker Adventist Hospital
Parker, Colorado
Juror Commendation, 2005 (AIA Dallas)

RadioShack Riverfront Campus
Fort Worth, Texas
*Brick in Architecture Award, 2005
(Brick Industry Association)*

RadioShack Riverfront Campus
Fort Worth, Texas
*Design Excellence Award, 2005 (IIDA Texas/
Oklahoma Chapter)*

RadioShack Riverfront Campus
Fort Worth, Texas
*Excellence in Design Award – Finalist, 2005
(Environmental Design & Construction)*

RadioShack Riverfront Campus
Fort Worth, Texas
Topping Out Award, 2005 (Dallas Business Journal)

Seminole County Criminal Justice Center
Sanford, Florida
*Architecture for Justice Knowledge Community – Justice
Facilities Review, 2005 (American Institute of Architects)*

Seminole County Criminal Justice Center
Sanford, Florida
*Orlando AIA Awards for Design Excellence, 2005
(AIA Orlando Chapter)*

South Jersey Regional Medical Center
Vineland, New Jersey
Healthcare Design Award, 2005 (The Center for Health Design)

The Center for American and International Law
Plano, Texas
Topping Out Award, 2005 (Dallas Business Journal)

The George Washington University Hospital
Washington, D.C.
Healthcare Design Award, 2005 (The Center for Health Design)

The Points at Waterview
Richardson, Texas
*TOBY Award/Office Building of the Year, 2005 (Building
Owners and Managers Association of America [BOMA])*

**University of Texas Southwestern Health
Science Center – Student Services and
Academic aministration Building**
San Antonio, Texas
*Golden Trowel Award, 2005 (San Antonio Masonry
Contractors Association)*

Washington Hospital Center ER One*
Washington, D.C.
*Award of Excellence, 2005 (AIA Modern Healthcare
Design Competition)*

Abbott Northwestern Heart Hospital
Minneapolis, Minnesota
Healthcare Design Award, 2006 (Center for Health Design)

**American British Cowdray Hospital
Oncology Center**
Mexico City, Mexico
Healthcare Design Award, 2006 (Center for Health Design)

Bayfront Medical Center – Surgery Expansion
St. Petersburg, Florida
Best of '06 Awards, 2006 (Southeast Construction)

Bayfront Medical Center – Surgery Expansion
St. Petersburg, Florida
*Excellence in Construction Award – Pyramid Winner,
2006 (ABC National)*

Blue Man Group Theatre
Las Vegas, Nevada
Design Award, 2006 (IIDA Texas/Oklahoma Chapter)

Clarian North Medical Center
Carmel, Indiana
Healthcare Design Award, 2006 (Center for Health Design)

Clarian North Medical Center
Carmel, Indiana
*Symposium Distinction Team Award, 2006
(Symposium on Healthcare Design)*

Clarian West Medical Center
Avon, Indiana
*Brick In Architecture Award, 2006 (Brick Industry
Association)*

Clarian West Medical Center
Avon, Indiana
Healthcare Design Award, 2006 (Center for Health Design)

CNL Tower II at City Commons
Orlando, Florida
*Golden Brick Award, 2006 (Downtown Orlando
Partnership)*

Dallas ISD Jesse Owens Memorial Complex

Dallas, Texas

Criteria Award – Design, Educational Appropriateness, 2006 (TASB/TASA Exhibit of School Architecture)

Dallas ISD Jesse Owens Memorial Complex

Dallas, Texas

Topping Out Award, 2006 (Dallas Business Journal)

Dell Diamond Ballpark

Round Rock (Austin), Texas

Best Minor League Ballpark, 2006 (Minor League News)

Garland Special Events Center

Garland, Texas

Architectural Portfolio, Citation, 2006 (American School & University)

Garland Special Events Center

Garland, Texas

Education Design Showcase, Honorable Mention, 2006 (School Planning & Management)

Garland Special Events Center

Garland, Texas

Topping Out Award, 2006 (Dallas Business Journal)

Hadassah Medical Center

Jerusalem, Israel

Citation, 2006 (AIA Modern Healthcare Design Competition)

Harris Methodist Fort Worth Hospital – Heart Center

Fort Worth, Texas

Award of Merit, 2006 (Brick Industry Association)

Orange County Library 3rd Floor Renovations

Orlando, Florida

Golden Brick Award, 2006 (Downtown Orlando Partnership)

Prairie View A&M University Architecture and Art Building

Prairie View, Texas

Award of Excellence – Higher Education, Design, 2006 (Texas Construction)

Texas Christian University GrandMarc at Westberry Place

Fort Worth, Texas

Best of 2006 – Multifamily, 2006 (Texas Construction)

Texas Scottish Rite Hospital for Children

Dallas, Texas

Dream Clients, 2006 (Building Design & Construction)

W Dallas - Victory Hotel and Residences

Dallas, Texas

Award of Excellence – Private/Hospitality, 2006 (Texas Construction)

W Dallas - Victory Hotel and Residences

Dallas, Texas

Best of 2006 – Private/Hospitality, Design, 2006 (Texas Construction)

W Dallas - Victory Hotel and Residences

Dallas, Texas

Topping Out Award, 2006 (Dallas Business Journal)

Walker Creek Elementary

North Richland Hills, Texas

Criteria Award – Design, Educational Appropriateness, Innovation, Process of Planning, 2006 (TASB/TASA Exhibit of School Architecture)

American Airlines Center Platinum Club

Dallas, Texas

Best of '07 Awards – Excellence Award, Renovation/ Restoration, Private, 2007 (Texas Construction)

American British Cowdray Hospital Oncology Center

Mexico City, Mexico

Honorable Mention, 2007 (Modern Healthcare Design Awards)

Children's Healthcare of Atlanta at Scottish Rite

Atlanta, Georgia

Design Award – Large Healthcare Category, 2007 (Contract)

Children's Healthcare of Atlanta at Scottish Rite

Atlanta, Georgia

Design Citation, 2007 (Georgia AIA)

Children's Healthcare of Atlanta at Scottish Rite

Atlanta, Georgia

Design of Excellence Award, 2007 (ASID Georgia Chapter)

Children's Healthcare of Atlanta at Scottish Rite

Atlanta, Georgia

Gold Award – Product/Custom Design (for donor wall), 2007 (ASID Georgia Chapter)

Children's Healthcare of Atlanta at Scottish Rite

Atlanta, Georgia

Healthcare Environment Award – Honorable Mention, 2007 (The Center for Health Design)

Children's Medical Center of Dallas – Ambulatory Care Pavilion

Dallas, Texas

Best of '07 Awards – Best of Award, Renovation/ Restoration, Health Care, 2007 (Texas Construction)

Dell Diamond Ballpark

Round Rock (Austin), Texas

Best Minor League Ballpark, 2007 (Minor League News)

Dickey Stephens Ballpark

North Little Rock, Arkansas

Best New Ballpark, 2007 (Ballparkdigest.com)

Dickey Stephens Ballpark

North Little Rock, Arkansas

Best New Ballpark, 2007 (Ballparks.com)

**Emory University Hospital Neuro
Critical Care Unit**

Atlanta, Georgia

Design Citation, 2007 (Society of Critical Care Medicine)

Garland Special Events Center

Garland, Texas

*Innovative Architecture and Design Award, 2007
(Recreation Management)*

Garland Special Events Center

Garland, Texas

*Paul Waterbury Award for Outdoor Lighting, 2007
(International Illumination Design)*

Glenn Clarke Condo

Dallas, Texas

Honorable Mention, 2007 (IIDA TX/OK Chapter)

Holmes Regional Medical Center

Melbourne, Florida

*Best of '07 Awards – Best Health Care, 2007
(Southeast Construction)*

Homestead Hospital

Homestead, Florida

*Best of '07 Awards – Award of Merit, 2007
(Southeast Construction)*

Corporate Office Building

Southfield, Michigan

Excellence in Architecture, 2007 (AIA Michigan)

Mainsail Development Group, LLC

Orlando, Florida

*Golden Brick Award, 2007 (Downtown Orlando
Partnership)*

Orange County Library 2nd Floor Renovations

Orlando, Florida

*Golden Brick Award, 2007 (Downtown Orlando
Partnership)*

Pizza Hut Park

Frisco, Texas

*Topping Out – Top Winner, 2007 (Dallas Business
Journal)*

**Presbyterian Hospital of Dallas,
Main Chapel Renovation**

Dallas, Texas

*Best of '07 Awards – Award of Merit, Renovation/
Restoration (Texas Construction)*

**Presbyterian Hospital of Dallas,
Main Chapel Renovation**

Dallas, Texas

Health Care, 2007 (Texas Construction)

St. Mary's/Duluth Clinic First Street Building

Duluth, Minnesota

*Excellence in Design – Finalist, 2007 (Environmental
Design + Construction)*

U.S. Census Bureau Headquarters

Suitland, Maryland

Design Award, 2007 (AIA Maryland)

W Dallas - Victory Hotel and Residences

Dallas, Texas

Honor Award – Large Project Category, 2007 (AIA Dallas)

W Dallas - Victory Hotel and Residences

Dallas, Texas

Hospitality Design Awards, 2007 (Hospitality Design)

Walker Creek Elementary

North Richland Hills, Texas

*Exhibition of School Architecture, 2007 (National School
Board Association)*

Washington Hospital Center ER One*

Washington, D.C.

Juror Commendation – Unbuilt, 2007 (AIA Dallas)

Ahuja Medical Center

Beachwood, Ohio

*Honorable Mention, Unbuilt Design Award, 2008
(Modern Healthcare Awards)*

Dell Diamond Ballpark

Round Rock (Austin), Texas

*Best Minor League Ballpark – Runner Up, 2008
(Minor League News)*

**Emory University Hospital Neuro
Critical Care Unit**

Atlanta, Georgia

*Build Georgia Award, 2008 (Associated General
Contractors, Georgia Branch)*

Florida Hospital East Orlando

Orlando, Florida

*Gold Award, 2008 (Construction Owners Association
of America)*

Garland Special Events Center

Garland, Texas

*Meeting Facility of the Year, 2008 (Meeting Professionals
International, Dallas/Fort Worth Chapter)*

Los Angeles Dodger Stadium Renovations

Los Angeles, California

L.A. Pride Award, 2008 (Los Angeles Business Council)

Lucas Oil Stadium

Indianapolis, Indiana

Overall Project of the Year, 2008 (Midwest Construction)

Phoenix Children's Hospital – NICU

Phoenix, Arizona

*Symposium Distinction Team Award, 2008 (Symposium
on Healthcare Design)*

Ritz-Carlton Hotel & Residences
Dallas, Texas
Topping Out Award, 2008 (Dallas Business Journal)

The Venetian Macao-Resort-Hotel*
Macau, China
Hospitality Design Award, 2008 (Hospitality Design)

W Hollywood Hotel & Residences
Hollywood, California
*Green Building Award, Unbuilt, 2008 (Los Angeles
Business Council)*

Walker Creek Elementary
North Richland Hills, Texas
Topping Out Award, 2008 (Dallas Business Journal)

Whataburger Field
Corpus Christi, Texas
Best Minor League Ballpark, 2008 (Minor League News)

**American British Cowdray Hospital Women's
and Children's Hospital**
Mexico City, Mexico
*Best International Health Project (over 40,000 sqm),
2009 (Design & Health International Academy Awards)*

Comprehensive Cancer Center
Wilmington, Delaware
*AIA Healthcare Design Awards – Unbuilt, 2009 (American
Institute of Architects)*

DFW International Airport Terminal D
Dallas/Fort Worth, Texas
*TSA Design Award – Built, 2009 (Texas Society
of Architects)*

Montage Beverly Hills
Beverly Hills, California
*Finalist – Luxury Public Spaces, 2009 (Hospitality
Design Awards)*

Phoenix Children's Hospital – NICU
Phoenix, Arizona
*RED Award – Honorable Mention, 2009 (Arizona
Commercial Real Estate Magazine)*

Tampa Port Authority Channelside Garage
Tampa, Florida
*Honor Award – Unbuilt Commercial Category, 2009
(AIA Orlando)*

Tampa Port Authority Channelside Garage
Tampa, Florida
*Merit Award for Architecture – Unbuilt Commercial
Category, 2009 (AIA Tampa)*

The Venetian Macao-Resort-Hotel*
Macau, China
*Hospitality Design Award – Finalist, Resort Design,
2009 (Hospitality Design)*

University of Texas Center for BrainHealth
Dallas, Texas
*TSA Design Award – Built, 2009 (Texas Society
of Architects)*

*Design in association with others.

Outstanding Architect Award 2000, 2001, 2002, 2003, 2004, 2005, 2006, 2007 (American Subcontractors Association/North Texas Chapter)

Modernization Award Honorable Mention, 2000 (Buildings)

Design Giant Award, 2001 (Interior Design Magazine's Survey of the Industry's Top Interior Design Firms)

Architecture Firm of the Year Award, 2002 (Texas Society of Architects)

Best Places to Work – Medium Size Business Category, 2003, 2004 (Dallas Business Journal)

Greater Dallas Business Ethics Award, Midsize Company, 2003 (Society of Financial Service Professionals/Dallas Chapter)

Momentum Dallas, Award of Merit, 2003 (Greater Dallas Chamber)

Best Companies to Work for in America, 2004 (Great Place to Work Institute/Society for Human Resource Management)

North Texas Best Family Friendly Companies, 2004 (Dallas Child and Fort Worth Child)

Best Bosses Award – Ralph Hawkins, Finalist 2005 (Fortune Small Business)

Graphic Design USA Awards, 2005 (Architecture for Healing, HKS website & INNOVATE magazine)

The Stevie Awards, Finalist, 2005 (The American Business Awards)

Best AEC Firm Site – Silver winner, 2006 (Building Design & Construction)

Best Companies to Work for in Texas, 2006 (Texas Monthly)

Breakthrough Award, 2006 (Facility Guidelines Institute)

CEO of the Year Award, 2006 (PSMJ Resources)

Financial Executive of the Year Award, Regional Winner, 2006 (Institute of Management Accountants/Robert Half International)

Graphic Design USA Awards, 2006 (INNOVATE magazine, HKS Regional Office Brochures (Phoenix & California), Twenty for Twenty Invitation, Atlanta Open House Invitation)

Best Places to Work – Large Size Business Category, 2007 (Dallas Business Journal)

Great Places to Work, 2007 (Richmond Magazine)

The Stevie Awards, Best Executive Business Services Category, 2007 (The American Business Awards)

Best Companies to Work for in Texas, 2008 (Texas Monthly)

Best Places to Work in Los Angeles, 2008, 2009 (Los Angeles Business Journal)

CFO of the Year – Finalist, 2008 (Dallas Business Journal)

The Stevie Awards, Best Finance Executive Category, 2008 (The American Business Awards)

Best AEC Firms to Work For, 2009 (Building Design + Construction)

Top 100 Places to Work, 2009 (The Dallas Morning News)

PHOTOGRAPHY CREDITS

Blake Marvin

American British Cowdray Cancer Center, 88–93

Atlantis Phase II, 192–193

Bassett Army Community Hospital, 66–69

Camelback Ranch, 246–249

Center for BrainHealth, 280–282

Cowboys Stadium, 206–209

Dodger Stadium, 226–227

Eastfield College Learning Center, 294–297

Four Seasons Hualalai, 154–157

Four Seasons Resort at Sharm el-Sheikh, 166–169

Four Seasons Scottsdale at Troon North, 184–189

Garland Special Events Center, 218–221

Hyatt Regency Tamaya, 174–175

Jersey Boys Theatre, 222–225

Loews Ventana Canyon Resort, 194–195

Lucas Oil Stadium, 210–215

Montage Laguna Beach, 148–151

Pizza Hut Park, 216–217

Shutters on the Beach, 146–147

St. Mary's/Duluth Clinic, 56–58

Suncadia, 180–183

The Palazzo Resort Hotel Casino, 49

The Ritz-Carlton, Bachelor Gulch, 176–179

The Ritz-Carlton, Half Moon Bay, 170–171

The Westin Kierland Resort and Spa, 172–173

Tucker's Point Club, 158–159

W Dallas – Victory Hotel & Residences, 140–143

Dan Ham

Hilton Orlando Convention Center Hotel, 196–197

Daryl Shields

Executive Committee and Management
   Council of Principals, 10

Ed LaCasse

Abbott Northwestern Heart Hospital, 100–103

Lynn Cancer Institute – Harvey & Phyllis Sandler
   Pavilion, 120–123

RadioShack Riverfront Campus, 42–47

Sabre Holdings Headquarters, 50–51, 54–55

Salem Hospital Regional Health Services, 114–119

St. Mary's/Duluth Clinic, 58–59

The Center for American and International Law, 324–325

Hyatt Regency Lost Pines Resort and Spa

Hyatt Lost Pines, 200–201

James Walshe

Jean-Michel Cousteau Fiji Islands Resort, 160–161

Joe Aker

Sabre Holdings Headquarters, 52–53

Justin Maconochie

Corporate Headquarters, 258–263

Ralph Cole Photography

Cowboys Stadium, 204–205

Richard Osbourne

Northern Batch Hope Hospital, 134–137

Rosewood Hotels & Resorts

Las Ventanas al Paraíso, 162–165

Scott Frances

Montage Beverly Hills, 144–145

The Venetian Macao-Resort-Hotel

The Venetian Macao-Resort-Hotel, 190–191

Tom Fox

Las Ventanas al Paraíso, 164

Robert Reck

Capella Pedregal, 152–153

DPR Construction, Inc.

Dodger Stadium, 227

INDEX

1000 Sunset Tower, 336

2006 HKS Design Fellowship Museum Tower, 342

2007 HKS Design Fellowship, 344

2008 HKS Design Fellowship, 346

Abbott Northwestern Heart Hospital, 100

Abu Dhabi Financial Centre – Luxury
  Hotel & Residences, 252

Academic Teaching Hospital, 304

Al Qudra Healthcare Medical Campus, 106

American British Cowdray Cancer Center, 88

Amon G. Carter Stadium Master Plan, 230

Atlantis Phase II, 192

Bassett Army Community Hospital, 66

Bayway Lofts, 328

Camelback Ranch, 246

Capella Pedregal, 152

Capital Health System Mercer Hospital, 30

Center for BrainHealth, 280

Charles E. Schmidt Medical Center – Master Plan, 308

Christus Muguerza Tuxtla Hospital, 104

Civica Plaza, 266

Comprehensive Cancer Center, 298

Corporate Office Building, 258

Cowboys Stadium, 204

D.C. United Soccer Stadium, 228

Danat Al Emarat Women's and Children's Hospital, 84

Dodger Stadium, 226

Dubai Cancer Center, 132

Eastfield College Learning Center, 294

Enze Medical Center, 94

Erbil Iraq Schools, 302

Estádio do Maracanã, 242

Federal University of Health Sciences, 80

Four Seasons Hualalai, 154

Four Seasons Resort at Sharm el-Sheikh, 166

Four Seasons Scottsdale at Troon North, 184

Garland Special Events Center, 218

Hall Arts Center, 264

Hall Financial Office Tower, 38

Hilton Orlando Convention Center Hotel, 196

Hyatt Lost Pines Resort and Spa, 200

Hyatt Regency Tamaya, 174

Jean-Michel Cousteau Fiji Islands Resort, 160

Jersey Boys Theatre, 222

JW Marriott San Antonio, 198

Karbala Teaching Hospital, 76

Kent Building Schools for the Future, 284

King Hussein Cancer Center, 128

Land_Scraper, 348

Las Ventanas al Paraíso, 162

Liverpool FC Stadium, 232

Loews Ventana Canyon Resort, 194

Lucas Oil Stadium, 210

Lynn Cancer Institute – Harvey & Phyllis
  Sandler Pavilion, 120

Milwaukee Palomar, 26

Montage Beverly Hills, 144

Montage Laguna Beach, 148

Museo del Niño – Parque Ecológico Chapultepec, 290

National Museum of Art, Architecture and Design, 352

National Taiwan University Cancer Center, 64

Nelson Mandela Children's Hospital, 62

Northern Batch Hope Hospital, 134

Northpark Center, 270

Phoenix Children's Hospital, 124

Pizza Hut Park, 216

Post Oak Mixed-Use Development, 256

Press Telegram Lofts, 332

Proposed 2014 World Cup Venue, 238

RadioShack Riverfront Campus, 42

Royal Children's Hospital, 110

Sabre Holdings Headquarters, 50

Salem Hospital Regional Health Services, 114

Shutters on the Beach, 146

Sonata, 330

St. Mary's/Duluth Clinic, 56

Statler Competition "A Temporary Facade," 354

Suncadia Lodge, 180

Ten10, 334

Terrace V, 274

Territorio Santos Modelo – Estadio Corona, 236

The Center for American and International Law, 324

The College of North West London, Wembley Campus, 314

The Palazzo Resort Hotel Casino, 48

The Ritz-Carlton, Bachelor Gulch, 176

The Ritz-Carlton, Half Moon Bay, 170

The Venetian Macao-Resort-Hotel, 190

The Westin Kierland Resort and Spa, 172

Tucker's Point Club, 158

UK Medical Centre for Research and Innovation, 318

University Hospitals Ahuja Medical Center, 70

University of Central Florida Physical Sciences Building, 288

Veleiro do Sul Skyscraper, 268

Vision Dallas, 16

W Dallas - Victory Hotel & Residences, 140

W Hollywood Hotel & Residences, 22

West End Pedestrian Bridge, 350

Woodruff Health Sciences Center, 34